EVERYTHING®

POCKET MOM

Dear Reader,

It's such an exciting time when your baby transitions
into an active toddler who is learning to walk, talk,
socialize, and be independent. As your child grows
up, you'll need to introduce him to so many things—
healthy sleep and play skills, toilet training, friendships,
and more! I've put together my best tips and techniques in *The Everything® Pocket Mom* to help guide
you on this journey.

One of the best ways to promote your toddler's
overall well-being is to offer him a variety of great-
tasting foods. Check out the fifty recipes in this book for
nutritious dishes that are simple and fun to make (let
your child help!) and packed with essential vitamins
and minerals.

Your toddler is probably the happiest when she's
busy exploring the world around her. That's why I've
also included dozens of easy, fun activities you can try
in a variety of places—inside, outside, or on the go!

Each new skill your child learns provides opportunities for you to further develop your parent-child
relationship. When you look back on these years,
somehow the challenges you and your child face
will pale in comparison to all the many, many joy-
ful, proud, and hilarious moments you experience
together.

Enjoy every (okay, almost every) moment!

Vincent Iannelli, MD

The **EVERYTHING** Series

These handy, accessible books give you all you need to tackle a difficult project, gain a new hobby, or even brush up on something you learned back in school but have since forgotten. You can read from cover to cover or just pick out information from our four useful boxes.

 Alerts: Urgent warnings

 Essentials: Quick handy tips

 Facts: Important snippets of information

 Questions: Answers to common questions

When you're done reading, you can finally say you know **EVERYTHING**®!

PUBLISHER Karen Cooper

DIRECTOR OF ACQUISITIONS AND INNOVATION Paula Munier

MANAGING EDITOR, EVERYTHING® SERIES Lisa Laing

COPY CHIEF Casey Ebert

ASSISTANT PRODUCTION EDITOR Jacob Erickson

ACQUISITIONS EDITOR Brett Palana-Shanahan

DEVELOPMENT EDITOR Laura Daly

EDITORIAL ASSISTANT Ross Weisman

EVERYTHING® SERIES COVER DESIGNER Erin Alexander

LAYOUT DESIGNERS Colleen Cunningham, Elisabeth Lariviere, Ashley Vierra, Denise Wallace

Visit the entire Everything® series at *www.everything.com*

THE
EVERYTHING®
POCKET
MOM

Quick and easy solutions for all
your parenting problems!

Vincent Iannelli, MD

Avon, Massachusetts

Published by
Adams Media, a division of F+W Media, Inc.
57 Littlefield Street, Avon, MA 02322. U.S.A.
www.adamsmedia.com

ISBN 10: 1-4405-3010-6
ISBN 13: 978-1-4405-3010-4
eISBN 10: 1-4405-3047-5
eISBN 13: 978-1-4405-3047-0

Printed in the United States of America.

10 9 8 7 6 5 4 3 2 1

Library of Congress Cataloging-in-Publication Data
is available from the publisher.

This book is intended as general information only, and should not be used to diagnose or treat any health condition. In light of the complex, individual, and specific nature of health problems, this book is not intended to replace professional medical advice. The ideas, procedures, and suggestions in this book are intended to supplement, not replace, the advice of a trained medical professional. Consult your physician before adopting any of the suggestions in this book, as well as about any condition that may require diagnosis or medical attention. The author and publisher disclaim any liability arising directly or indirectly from the use of this book.

This publication is designed to provide accurate and authoritative information with regard to the subject matter covered. It is sold with the understanding that the publisher is not engaged in rendering legal, accounting, or other professional advice. If legal advice or other expert assistance is required, the services of a competent professional person should be sought.

—From a *Declaration of Principles* jointly adopted
by a Committee of the American Bar Association and
a Committee of Publishers and Associations

Many of the designations used by manufacturers and sellers to distinguish their product are claimed as trademarks. Where those designations appear in this book and Adams Media was aware of a trademark claim, the designations have been printed with initial capital letters.

This book is available at quantity discounts for bulk purchases.
For information, please call 1-800-289-0963.

Contents

Introduction

Let's face it: No parent has the time to pour over the hundreds of child development books on the market today, which often contradict each other or simply push the latest parenting fad. Does that mean you and your child have to struggle with every difficult phase, rocky transition, and parenting dilemma that comes your way? No—you only need this book, your ultimate resource for surviving key childhood milestones, from weaning off a bottle to going potty to starting kindergarten.

Once you're out of the bleary-eyed babyhood phase, most aspects of parenting become more fun for moms and dads. Your child may be talking, making friends, or developing interesting personality traits and passions. He may love eating scrambled eggs just like his dad, or doing jigsaw puzzles like his mom. She may delight in reading bedtime stories with her mom, or playing baseball with her dad. Hand in hand with these developments, however, come the inevitable challenges—ear-piercing tantrums, refusing to share, or stubbornly avoiding the potty. But past each age-appropriate obstacle is a triumph you can both enjoy, and that's why toddlerhood can be one of the most awe-inspiring and magical times in the lives of both parent and child. All you need is a little direction to change these often trying years into terrific memories.

As the parent of a young child, you have a unique role and opportunity. Studies show that early home life and experiences have the strongest impact on a child's development and future success. You can add fun, learning, and enrichment to your child's life every day with your ability to set and enforce limits, model good behavior, and maintain a healthy lifestyle. The information in this book will develop and strengthen the bond between you and your child. And at the end of the (exhausting) day, isn't that what you want most?

PART I

Your Growing Child

CHAPTER 1

Mealtimes and More

As your baby moves into the toddler years, you have an opportunity to set in place some good eating habits that will be healthy for later years. If your baby has eaten a wide range of healthy foods, it is likely that the shift to foods from the family menu will not be difficult, although some toddlers go through a phase of being a little picky. It's not unusual for a toddler to want to eat one food for breakfast, lunch, and dinner!

Weaning from the Breast or Bottle

Cultures vary tremendously in the area of weaning a baby or toddler from breastfeeding. Western societies tend to frown on nursing "too long," although that is changing in recent decades. Generally it is up to you and your toddler to wean when you decide to wean. Even the American Academy of Pediatrics states that there is no upper limit to the duration of breastfeeding. Your toddler may become bored with it and gradually taper off, though. Or you may go back to work and need to adjust when and if you nurse because of new lifestyle commitments. However and whenever it occurs, it is your own business.

For bottle-fed babies, it is important to wean off the bottle by twelve to eighteen months. Children who continue to use bottles are more likely to experience tooth decay, even at this young age.

Quick Weaning Tips

You can soften the blow in the following ways:

- Choose a time when the child isn't coping with other major stresses.
- Tell your child you are going to wean him.
- Provide milk in a cup with meals.
- Nurse after meals, when the child has less of an appetite.
- Eliminate one bottle or nursing session at a time, beginning with the one the child is least attached to—typically in the middle of the day.

- Avoid the cues that trigger the desire to be nursed or have a bottle by staying busy or sitting in a different chair.
- Spend the time you would have devoted to nursing reading a story, reciting nursery rhymes, or playing together.
- Offer bottle-fed babies a bottle of water.
- Wait five days before eliminating a second bottle or nursing session.
- Eliminate bedtime feedings last. (Provide other kinds of comfort until the child learns to fall asleep without being nursed. If possible, have Dad handle bedtime.)

🅴❗ Alert

If you continue to nurse past age two or three, you will need to teach your toddler some specific ways of asking to nurse. He will need to learn that there are situations where it will be comfortable for you and others where he will have to wait for a while. It still is the mother's body, even though shared, and you may need to assert some boundaries so you're not embarrassed in a playgroup or social situation.

Introducing a Cup

As you wean your baby off the breast or bottle, you'll need to introduce him to a cup as a replacement. Begin to introduce the cup between six and nine months of age.

Babies develop the ability to move objects from hand to hand in the middle of their bodies (midline) at around six months. By nine months, this skill is well mastered and babies are ready to manipulate cups with lids.

Expect the cup to become a new toy for your baby. He'll throw it and expect you to pick it up (over and over and over). This game is not played to frustrate you. Your baby is learning cause and effect ("If I throw it, you'll pick it up . . . every time!") and object permanence (the cup still exists even though he couldn't see it for a minute). Both of these concepts are important for normal development, and you've provided the right age-appropriate toy to teach them.

Five Squares a Day?

As your baby eats more and more solid foods, it's natural to struggle with how much to feed her and when. Toddlers have a reputation for being finicky eaters, but the truth is that their growth rate is slowing down at this stage. They are developmentally becoming quite skilled in various aspects of their being, but they are not adding very many pounds between eighteen months and three years. That's why you don't need to push big quantities of food on little ones. Instead, offer five small meals a day, emphasizing finger foods.

Toddlers need about 1,100 to 1,300 calories per day, proportionately from the various food groups. Large, active children will need a little more, and smaller, sedentary toddlers will need fewer. Calorie counting gets tricky, especially when half of everything that goes onto toddlers' plates ends up on their clothes or on the floor. Realistically, counting calories usually isn't necessary if your toddler is growing well. You may find it easier to think in terms of the number of servings. In general, if you're offering a wide array of nutritious foods, and your child eats enough to be full and happy, she's doing fine.

Essential Food Groups

Only a few generalities are certain when it comes to feeding your family: fresh foods are better than processed; pesticide-free food is healthier. So try to take up cooking! The typical American diet consists of so much poor-quality food, most of which you can avoid if you prepare meals yourself. If cooking is too difficult to fit into your family's schedule, be sure to read labels to figure out which packaged goods are healthy choices.

The first thing chefs need to know is that besides supplying vitamins, minerals, and other ingredients needed for good health (such as fiber), foods provide energy. Energy is measured in calories. Calories, which are measured in grams, come from three sources: proteins, fats, and sugars. Children need all three kinds. However, you do not need to be a scientist to make sure your child's meals are nutritious. Common sense goes a long way toward serving your toddler (and your family) nutritious meals. In addition, the United States Department of Agriculture's easy-to-read plate diagram shows you the quantities needed within each food group according to the age and needs of the person. The food groups are as follows:

- Grains
- Vegetables
- Fruits
- Dairy
- Protein

An extra category includes snacks, oil, beverages, salt, and sugar. The site at *www.choosemyplate.gov/* offers an interactive page for parents of young children. You can even enter your toddler's age, level of exercise, and special needs and receive information about nutrition.

Grains

Bread, rice, cereal, and pasta, which are made primarily or wholly from grains, provide energy from complex carbohydrates. Parents should provide six to eleven servings per day. One toddler serving equals:

- ¼ to ½ slice whole-grain bread
- ¼ cup dry cereal
- ¼ English muffin
- ¼ cup cooked pasta or rice (brown or wild is best)
- ¼ whole-grain bagel

- 2 to 3 whole-wheat crackers
- ¼ cup hot cereal

Unrefined grains (such as whole-wheat bread) are healthier than highly refined grains (such as white bread), even if the manufacturer says that nutrients are put back into the product. Remember that at least half of all grain servings should be whole grains.

Vegetables

Vegetables contain protein, but they make up their own food group. Also, what makes vegetables so important are the vitamins and fiber they contain. Some of the vitamins are lost in the canning process, so fresh is always better. The recommended daily allowance (RDA) charts on packaged foods list how much of needed vitamins and other nutrients foods contain. Keep these points in mind:

1. Frozen vegetables are better than canned, since fewer vitamins are lost in processing. Vegetables lightly steamed in cookware with a tight-fitting lid are better still. Raw vegetables are best of all.
2. Starchy vegetables like potatoes and yams are especially rich in nutrients, but they become a less-than-great choice when fat—butter, cheese, gravy, sour cream, or oil—is added.
3. Beans, which are rich in vitamins and fiber as well as protein, can meet vegetable or protein requirements.

4. A toddler serving is usually equal to about 1 to 2 tablespoons of cooked vegetables.

Fruit

Fruit—including fresh, dried, frozen, and home-squeezed into juice—is rich in vitamins, especially vitamin C. Beware of fruit canned in sugary syrup, and juices that contain mostly sugar and only a squirt of real fruit juice. A few drops can result in a label that proclaims in large letters, "Contains real juice!" The question is how much juice, and you must read the label to find out.

Offer two or more servings of fruit per day. One serving equals approximately 1 tablespoon per year of life, so two-year-olds need at least 4 tablespoons per day. The equivalent is:

- ½ cup (4 ounces) of juice
- ½ piece of whole fruit

Dairy/Protein

Protein, which is essential for good nutrition, comes from meats, poultry, fish, eggs, nuts, and beans. It's the extras—the skin and fat or addition of oil for frying, butter for baking, and cream sauces for smothering—that quickly add to the calories from fat. Milk, cheese, and yogurt are also high in protein and are rich sources of another essential nutrient, calcium. Low-fat products are preferable for children over age two because they have fewer calories from fat. Provide two to four toddler servings of meat and high-protein alternatives daily, and three to four servings of milk, yogurt, and cheese. One toddler serving equals:

- ½ whole egg or 1 white
- ¼ cup baked beans
- ¾ cup milk
- 3 slices turkey luncheon meat
- ¼ cup nonfat dry milk
- ¾ ounce hard cheese
- ⅓ cup yogurt
- 1 ounce poultry, meat, or fish
- 3 tablespoons cottage cheese
- 1 tablespoon smooth peanut butter

Other Components of Healthy Eating

In addition to the main food groups, you'll want to be sure you offer your toddler other components of a healthy diet, such as fat, fiber, calcium, the proper amount of liquids, and a range of vitamin-packed foods.

Fat

When it comes to calories from fat, the problem is usually keeping children from getting too much, especially after age two—processed foods tend to be loaded with it. But don't let round tummies and folds of baby fat fool you. Toddlers are supposed to be roly-poly. They'll eventually lose their round toddler belly. For now, serve whole milk to ensure they get enough fat (once they turn two, make the switch to skim or low-fat milk). Keep in mind that some kids can make the switch to low-fat milk even earlier—such as at their first birthday—if they are overweight or are at risk of becoming overweight. Toddlers don't need low-fat diets unless there's a special reason!

Don't Forget Fiber

Fiber is important for proper functioning of the bowels. Hefty portions serve as an antidote for chronic constipation. Offer three or more servings of vegetables per day. One serving equals approximately 1 tablespoon per year of life, so two-year-olds need at least 6 tablespoons per day. Besides raw vegetables, other high-fiber foods include whole-grain breads and cereals, beans and peas, and fruit.

Calcium Counts

Calcium is required for bone growth, so to ensure your child gets enough calcium, you will need to provide daily doses. Good choices include cow's milk, calcium-fortified orange juice, calcium-fortified soymilk, canned sardines or salmon (with the bones), fortified goat's milk, kale, tofu, and turnip greens.

Liquids

Toddlers probably need 4 to 6 cups of liquids daily under normal circumstances—more in hot weather or if they are ill with fever, vomiting, or diarrhea. Besides fluoridated water (from the tap or bottled, plain or carbonated), good sources of liquids include soup, 100 percent fruit or vegetable juices, and milk.

Vitamins

If your toddler is eating a wide variety of foods, you probably do not need to fret about giving him a vitamin. Nature tends to take care of itself if you are offering (and your child is eating) many foods from different food groups.

 Fact

All calories are not created equal! A calorie from a substantial grain or vegetable genuinely nourishes a child. A calorie from a sugary food or drink is empty. It does nothing to contribute to a child's health. Too many extra calories from fat and sugar sources can result in a weight problem. Soda, too much juice, and sugary breakfast cereals are common sources of extra sugar. Avoid them to keep your toddler healthy and to help her develop good eating habits.

In general, your toddler should be sure to eat foods rich in vitamin D, calcium, and iron each day, in addition to other important vitamins and minerals, such as vitamin A, vitamin C, and fluoride. Unless your toddler is extremely picky, has a chronic medical problem, or is missing out on one or more food groups, he is likely getting all the vitamins and minerals he needs from his diet and doesn't need an extra vitamin supplement. Talk to your pediatrician if you think your child does need a vitamin. He or she can make sure you give one that includes what your child is actually missing in his diet.

Healthy Food, Happy Toddler

As much as possible, steer your toddler away from junk foods. Learn to read labels in the supermarket. If the ingredients include lots of substances you can't pronounce, look for a healthier version of that item instead. Many already prepared foods include large amounts of added sugar, and too much of it alters your child's taste preferences, setting up a dynamic for later eating difficulties.

 **Essential**

Growing your own vegetables is wonderful for your family, including your toddler. There is nothing like firsthand knowledge of digging the hole, putting in the seed, watering it, watching for the first leafy shoots, and then pulling up the carrot and eating it! Children who participate in gardening truly understand that food comes from the earth, not just from the store.

Whole Foods

The easiest way to ensure that you know what's in the food you eat is to make it yourself. Organic foods from your natural food store or farmers' market and other whole foods are much healthier for everyone in your family, including your little one.

At its core, whole food is food that has been grown and produced as close as possible to the way that nature intended, without being processed. In addition, organic food is grown without the aid of pesticides, herbicides, or synthetic fertilizers. Because organic livestock does not receive routine doses of antibiotics, the animals have living conditions that promote good health, including adequate space, fresh air, fresh water, and healthy feed. Furthermore, genetically modified organisms (GMOs), synthetic hormones, and irradiation are not allowed in organic agricultural products. Not only is organic food grown in accordance with organic practices, but the organic commitment also continues all the way from field to store.

Since 2002, the United States Department of Agriculture (USDA) has overseen the national organic program in the United States. The USDA has instituted an extensive set of rules that dictate what is allowable and what is prohibited in organic agricultural products for food and nonfood use. The USDA also oversees third-party certifiers, which ensure that the rules are followed by organic producers.

Make Good Food Interesting

You probably don't have to work very hard to get your child to eat a cookie. Fruits and veggies, on the other hand, may require some creative thinking. Check out Appendix A for delicious recipes for mealtime and snacktime. Here are a few other ideas you can try:

- Cut bread with cookie cutters to create interesting shapes before topping with cheese or vegetables. Freeze the scraps and use them later to stuff chicken or turkey.
- Slice a banana lengthwise to make a boat, stand a piece of sliced cheese inside to make a sail, and float it in a pool of blueberry yogurt. You can even infest the water with shark fins made from salami slices. (If that combination doesn't sound appealing to you, remember that your child probably won't mind, and it all ends up in the same place, anyway!)
- Spread strips of toast with cream cheese or peanut butter and top with a row of raisins for an enticing dish of "ants on a log."
- Make pancakes topped with fruit strategically placed to resemble facial features.

The first few times tots taste peas, broccoli, and any number of other foods parents consider healthy, it is common for them to turn up their noses and vigorously shake their heads, or even spit out the food. After trying again and again, the best recourse, nutritionists say, is for parents to try yet again and again. It can take eight to ten exposures before a youngster develops a taste for a new food.

Picky Eaters

Many toddlers turn out to dislike certain foods. That's only natural. Just as many adults don't like liver or escargot, your toddler will evolve certain definite preferences. Some toddlers are downright picky. What can you do in those situations? Here are two options.

 **Essential**

Encourage your child to help you fix these healthy meals and snacks! She may be more likely to eat the good food if she's helped you prepare it. When you're cooking, especially if it's a shared time with your toddler, turn off the phone, television, music, and computer.

The first way is to eliminate all food struggles by serving what your child wants, as long as it isn't a lot of extra milk, juice, or junk food. If a war for control is driving the resistance, catering to toddler demands eliminates the toddler's need to battle over food. If your doctor says it's okay, supplement his diet with vitamins, some fortified milk, and a cup of fruit or vegetable juice to maintain nutrition. Continue to make other foods available by placing them on his plate if he'll allow them to be there, or place them on a separate plate nearby, but don't force him to try everything you give him. If both of those create upset, simply follow your normal serving procedures for the rest of the family.

If your toddler does request something additional, dish out a serving. Studiously avoid questions about whether he likes it and comments about being glad that he's eaten something besides the usual. The goal is to not draw attention to his eating or make an issue of it, thereby preventing a basis for renewed resistance. Keep in mind that some toddlers only eat one full meal a day and will just pick at the other meals, and that can be normal, as long as he isn't filling up on extra less-nutritious calories.

 **Question**

When should I try to give my toddler new foods?
When your toddler (even your picky one!) is in a growth spurt, he may be more receptive to new foods. Offer them early in the meal, when he's more likely to be hungry.

The second way is to ignore the child's demands, serve what you will, and wait until hunger motivates him to eat. The refusal to eat a well-balanced meal often stems from snacking. Some toddlers restrict their diets to the point that it seems that if it were up to them, they'd only eat one or two things—such as grilled cheese sandwiches, fish crackers, hamburgers, or a particular type of cereal—three meals a day, every day. "If I don't fix what he wants, he won't eat anything," his parent claims. But how true is that, really? Limit snacks and your child may eat better at meals. Understand that food jags, in which a toddler only wants a certain type of food for several days or weeks, are not uncommon, though.

Mealtime Misbehaving

Most toddlers occasionally throw food or act up during mealtimes. As with many toddler behaviors, you should do your best to avoid situations that will exacerbate this problem and try to stick to a routine for mealtimes. If your toddler is hungry and her meal isn't ready, give her a small, healthy snack to hold her over. If possible, don't put your toddler in her high chair or booster seat until the meal is ready. If you must put her in there beforehand, give her several activities (books to look at, cars to race, a doll to talk to) to keep her entertained in the meantime. Most toddlers will only sit in one place for about twenty minutes, so keep your expectations realistic.

 Alert

Toddlers, like adults, will eat out of boredom. If the parent responds to requests for a snack by offering several healthy alternatives but the child refuses anything but a cookie, she's probably not hungry. An appealing activity or nap may do a better job of eliminating the crankiness.

If your toddler has a particularly tough time, keep in mind that toddlers must be simultaneously nurtured (by being fed) and given firm limits (by restraining them in a high chair and keeping them from throwing food). Balancing the two is a heady emotional experience, but in most cases mealtime behavior issues are a phase—a frustrating one, but a phase nonetheless. See Chapter 4 for more information on setting and enforcing limits, and create a few rules that will promote a fun but functional eating environment.

Enjoying Dining Out with a Toddler

Toddlers can make very unpleasant dining companions in restaurants because dining out requires two skills they haven't yet mastered: sitting and waiting. Taking them to places designed for adults is apt to be a miserable experience for the parents, the child, and other patrons as well. At this stage, restaurants are not likely to be a place where you can relax and enjoy yourself.

You can minimize upsets, however, by arriving prepared. In general, the more upscale the restaurant, the longer the wait to eat; so if the cupboard in your diaper bag is bare, don't even wait for the waiter—as you're being seated, ask the host to bring bread or crackers immediately. In addition, try to visit restaurants at nonpeak times so your wait time is lessened.

Of course, it's a good idea to arrive with entertainment, too. Try to bring a small toy or book that's new and different; otherwise, the novelty of items on the table will hold much more appeal. This might be the time to introduce a new app on your iPad. Rather than beginning the litany of no-nos the minute a small hand gravitates toward a coffee cup, scan the table for items your toddler can safely play with. Trying to prevent youngsters from touching *everything* guarantees a series of noisy scenes. Toddlers simply must have something to do, so be realistic. Allow them to shred a napkin or to bang a spoon if there's a tablecloth to dampen the sound.

CHAPTER 2

Potty Training

If you feel nervous about potty training, it may be because the very word *training* conjures images of housebreaking a pet or you have heard horror stories from other parents. For this reason, many parenting experts want to eliminate the phrase *potty training* altogether. For toddlers it is *potty learning*. Your job will be to serve as coach to work out a game plan and supervise short, simple practice sessions; as a teacher to provide instruction; and as a cheerleader to nurture a can-do attitude.

Communicating Instructions

Are you wondering how to communicate with babies and toddlers who don't understand much of what you say, and don't speak very well, if at all? Fortunately, youngsters understand more than they can verbalize. Still, you must take special steps to help make sure they understand what you are trying to say.

- **Get your child's full attention before speaking.** If you tell your child to go to the potty and get no response, she may not have even realized that you were talking to her. Always begin by saying your child's name. Don't continue until she looks up.
- **Tell your child what to do rather than what not to do.** Sentences containing negative words (such as "don't") are harder to grasp. To comprehend "don't stand up," children must understand "stand up" first, and then understand that "don't" means they are to do the opposite. That's too confusing! "Sit down" is much clearer.
- **Combine words with gestures.** Point to the bathroom when you tell your child to go there. Pat the potty when telling her to sit down on the potty. Children learn by hearing words combined with visual signals.
- **Use consistent language.** It's hard enough for a youngster to learn, "Go to the potty." She may not also understand, "Let mama take you to the bathroom," "Come with me to the potty," "Let's take

you to the potty," "Let's get you into the toilet fast." Choose a single set of words and phrases, and stick to them!

- **Show toddlers exactly what to do by modeling the behavior.** Put a stuffed animal on the potty. Enlist a willing sibling or parent to give a demonstration, or use a doll that wets. Read storybooks about potties.
- **Combine verbal instructions with manual guidance.** Place your hands on your child's shoulders and apply gentle pressure while telling her to sit on the potty. Cover her hands with yours to help her remove her pants. Show her what to do while you tell her.

Combining verbal, visual, and physical direction helps children learn new vocabulary and enhances communication. To be a good teacher, use every means at your disposal to help your little student understand what she's to do!

Providing Feedback

To coach effectively, you need to give children lots of feedback to help them understand what is happening. There are three kinds of feedback.

1. **Neutral feedback** is a straightforward statement that gives youngsters information about what they are doing, for example, "You're urinating." This kind of basic information is important for children who have always worn diapers and don't even realize when they are passing waste.

2. **Positive feedback** informs students about what they are doing correctly so they know to repeat it, for example, "Great! You're urinating in the potty!"

3. **Negative feedback** tells them what they are doing wrong, as in "Oh, no! You're urinating in your pants!" If you do give negative feedback, be sure to tell your child how to correct the mistake: "Oh no! You're urinating in your pants! You should do that in the potty next time."

Some toddlers are bolder and more confident than others. They may not learn anything from negative feedback, but they aren't especially daunted by it, either. Other children are far more sensitive. Even a hint that they are doing something wrong destroys their confidence, and they give up. They need lots of positive feedback to stay motivated!

Is Your Child Ready?

Although many toddlers are ready to start potty training between eighteen months and two years, in order to be potty trained, children must be physically capable of controlling their bladders and bowels. Your child should also be well rested, physically up to par, and emotionally ready to tackle a new skill. If your toddler is under the weather or preoccupied with other problems, let him choose whether he wants to wear diapers or underpants. Most important, always remember that learning to use the potty should be a good experience for everyone, so back off or get help once it isn't anymore. Physically, a child who is ready may:

- Remain dry for three to four hours at a time.
- Awaken from a nap with a dry diaper.
- Pass a substantial quantity of urine at one time.
- Have bowel movements at predictable times.
- Routinely go to a specific place to urinate or have a bowel movement while still in a diaper (e.g., a corner of the living room).
- Understand the purpose of the toilet (that he goes to the bathroom there).
- Tell when their bladder is full (recognize the physical sensation of the urge to urinate).
- Recognize the urge to have a bowel movement (recognize the physical sensation of the urge to pass stool).

In addition, watch for emotional signs that your child may be ready to start potty training. He might:

- Be proud of his accomplishments.
- Enjoy independence.
- Want to wear underwear.
- Dislike wet or soiled diapers.
- Be able to sit quietly for five minutes.
- Be undistracted by other major stresses.
- Have a good relationship with adults he wants to please.

If your child is interested in learning about the potty, let him help you pick out a potty to use. Let the new potty sit in the bathroom for several days so your child becomes accustomed to seeing it. Let him carry it around the house and play with it in his own way. Unless he can't wait to try it, have him sit on it fully clothed several times before trying it bare-bottomed. That way, he can adjust to sitting low to the ground on a chair with a hole in the middle before experiencing the cold seat. It's better to move too slowly than too fast!

 Alert

Praise is a type of positive feedback that communicates, "I am proud that you did that." Praise can help children feel good about themselves, build confidence, and motivate them to repeat certain behaviors. However, when toddlers are grappling with independence issues, they sometimes feel compelled to do the exact opposite of what parents want. So instead of gushing, "You used the potty! Mommy's so proud of you," try offhand comments such as, "Aren't you proud of yourself?" or "You should be proud."

If your child doesn't even attempt to sit on the potty when instructed, set him up to succeed and then give positive feedback instead of criticizing. For instance, place a teddy bear on the potty and praise it. Ask your child to pat the bear's head, and praise your child if he does by saying, "Yes! Teddy likes that!"

Effective Rewards

Rewards for making progress on the potty must be sufficiently enjoyable to outweigh children's reluctance to go to the potty. Pleasing a parent matters lots to most children, so hugs and kisses and other expressions of approval may keep them motivated. Spending one-on-one time with you will feel like a great reward, so when you accompany your youngster to the bathroom and serve as an attentive audience, your presence can provide a powerful incentive.

 Question

> **Should I punish my child if he does not use the potty when I think she is ready?**
> No. Threats or punishment during potty training can backfire dramatically. Fear mobilizes children's inborn fight-or-flight impulse. The child may not fight back or flee at the time, but will start avoiding the potty, and her aggressive behavior toward siblings, peers, pets, parents, or caregivers may increase.

Anyone who has ever tried to diet knows how difficult it is to practice self-denial today to reap a reward in a month or two. Therefore, a good reward is something your child can enjoy immediately. Promises of a chance to put a quarter in a grocery store gumball machine tomorrow, to hear an extra bedtime story later in the evening, or to receive a special toy in a week do not motivate most children. It's more effective to offer an on-the-spot hug, sticker, or story.

Sometimes stickers, small toys, treats, or special privileges can also reduce demands on parents' time. Providing tangible evidence of the child's accomplishment can help instill pride in a job well done, and by doling out rewards, parents remain involved without having to spend so much time sitting in the bathroom with their child. However, some experts point out that playing into toddler greed and giving prizes instead of attention warps children's values. A preprinted smiley face is no substitute for a parent's smiling face. If you give treats and toys, it's important to give positive attention, too.

Modeling

Children relish doing what friends and other family members do. If toddlers regularly see parents using the toilet, they are likely to want to copy them. Saying that using the potty makes him a "big boy" just like an idolized parent, or older sibling, friend, or relative can motivate them! Because children attending day care centers have many opportunities to observe and mimic more accomplished peers, they often master potty training earlier than stay-at-home peers. Similarly, younger siblings learn more quickly if older brothers, sisters, and/or parents allow them to watch. Let your child watch you use the bathroom or find someone else who is willing to serve as a model.

Unfortunately, the prospect of becoming a big boy doesn't always strike toddlers as appealing. While little folks sometimes enjoy the greater freedom, independence, autonomy, and respect that come with using the potty, at other times they grasp the downside—they are saddled with big responsibilities. Big people do less for them and expect them to do more for themselves. In fact, the pressures for increased maturity inherent in potty training often cause children to stop progressing or to regress in other areas. Parents can help toddlers overcome their ambivalence about growing up by reducing demands in other areas, tolerating more clinging, and providing extra doses of TLC.

 **Essential**

Reward potty progress with a special phone call to Grandma Lois, Uncle Mark, Cousin David, or any family friend willing to "ooh" and "ah" over the latest victory. Put your child on the line, or be sure he listens in as you share the good news. This means a lot to little folks.

Beginning Potty Practice

After watching your child carefully and noting the times at which she eats and eliminates on a calendar, schedule one or more daily potty practices when your child is likely to need to have a bowel movement. Some children regularly have a bowel movement a half hour or so after eating, regardless of when they eat. When your child doesn't object to sitting on the potty without a diaper, begin generating excitement for the big event. Announce that she will wear pull-ups and learn to use the potty just like Mommy/

Daddy/big brother/big sister and all the big kids at day care. Choose a time when she is in a good mood, rested, and healthy.

Several Daily Practices

Hold potty practice when you expect your child to have a bowel movement. If she is too irregular to predict, set up a regular schedule: When your schedule permits, hold potty practice first thing in the morning, shortly after breakfast, midmorning or immediately after a morning nap, shortly after lunch, midafternoon or immediately after her afternoon nap, shortly after dinner, and before bed. Although you should try to schedule practices around bowel movements, more frequent sessions give her more opportunities to urinate in the potty, too. Busy dual-income families and single working parents can ask day care providers to have their youngster spend five minutes in the bathroom at likely times or at regular two-hour intervals.

Take her to the bathroom shortly before you expect her to have a bowel movement and close the door. Put a small piece of toilet paper in the potty so that if she urinates just a tiny bit, you will be able to tell by looking at the paper and can congratulate her. Show her how to pull her pants and pull-ups down to her ankles, bending at the knees so she doesn't fall. Have her sit all the way back on the potty chair with the legs slightly spread so you can see and point out what is happening if she begins urinating.

First "Success"

If your child begins eliminating unexpectedly when she isn't sitting on the potty, tell her to try to stop. Few toddlers know how to stop once they've started, but at least she'll know it's possible, and it's important to start teaching the lesson that she should go to the potty whenever she is passing waste. If she does stop, say, "Good girl!" and guide her to the potty fast.

Have an extra bowl within easy reach so that if she has the usual toddler reaction of being still and watching herself urinate, you can try to catch some urine in the extra bowl and pour it into her potty bowl to show her where it's supposed to go. When she is through admiring it, help her pour it into the toilet "so it can go bye-bye with Mama's urine." Invite her to flush, but if she doesn't respond, flush after she has left the room. The violence of the swirling water upsets some children.

She's Learning!

Your child has now been through the entire process and should have a better idea as to what's involved even if she didn't have a bowel movement and didn't make it to the potty when she urinated. Hold practice sessions regularly, about once every two hours, and try to have her sit on the potty for five minutes each time. When she notifies you that she needs to use the potty or starts taking herself, you may not need to hold regular practice sessions unless she gets distracted and doesn't go when there are more fun things to do.

If Nothing Happens

If your child doesn't urinate or have a bowel movement during her first potty practice session, she either didn't need to use it or was too tense to go. Begin holding regular potty practice sessions timed to coincide with when you expect she might need to go, and have her spend three to five minutes practicing relaxing.

 Fact

When it comes to deciding when and where to go to the bathroom, all the punishments and praise and presents you offer may not make much of a difference. For once, toddlers are in control. All you can do is teach children what they need to know to be able to use the potty, help them acquire the specific skills, try to increase their motivation, and remain confident that if nothing else, the social pressures of kindergarten (if not preschool and day care) will provide an incentive powerful enough to zap the thorniest resistance.

If she protests strongly about having to stay in the bathroom, remain calm, but don't let a temper tantrum ruin your attempts at potty training. If you have to force your child to stay in the bathroom, she may not be ready or you may be taking her too often. You might try again when she is in a better mood or back off for a few weeks.

Even if your timing is good and your child remains seated on the potty during the practices, she may still be too tense to go. Don't be surprised if she soils or wets as soon as he stands up or shortly after the practice session ends and her diaper is back on. This is normal. The sphincter won't open until she relaxes. Tell her she can try again later, clean her up, wait about two hours, and hold another potty practice. Until she can comfortably remain seated for five minutes, devote the sessions to helping her relax.

 Fact

> Whenever your child has a potty practice session, tell her that she must relax before she can use the potty. Keep your focus positive by noting anything she does *right* as she works on relaxing: "Your arms are resting now. That's a good way to relax." Help her relax by making the time pleasant, too. Sit next to her on the floor while she sits on the potty and read her a book, sing a song together, or recite nursery rhymes. Children have a hard time relaxing and sitting still if they have a lot of pent-up energy. Provide time for active play before each potty practice session.

If she uses the potty, have her empty and rinse the potty bowl and wash her hands. If she has an accident shortly before a practice session, hold it anyway if you think she would benefit from practicing sitting on the potty and relaxing.

Tricks and Tactics

It's amazing how a single trick can capture toddlers' imagination and provide a permanent motivational fix. In addition, these tactics can help recondition the sphincters so they can open instead of remaining closed as long as possible whenever your child's bottom is bare.

- **Sail the Ping-Pong ball.** Drop a Ping-Pong ball in the toilet bowl and let toddler boys sail it as they spray. It will help them learn to aim before firing. Wash your hands after retrieving it!
- **Bull's eye.** Draw a magic marker target on a piece of tissue paper and drop it in the potty or toilet bowl and see if your little boy can score a hit.
- **Sink or swim?** Float a piece of paper towel in the toilet bowl and see if your toddler can sink it. Improve his aim by using progressively smaller pieces.
- **Firefighter.** Suggest your toddler don his firefighter hat and douse the imaginary blaze raging in the toilet with his urine. That means, of course, that he will have to go fast if he's to save the house from ruin. Next time he's wiggling about, don't yell, "Go to the potty *now*!" Just yell, "*Fire!*"
- **Gardener.** Paint flowers inside the potty bowl or affix stickers featuring flowers. Alternatively, cut the flower designs off of printed paper towels and drop them into the toilet. Then, declare the "garden" in need of a sprinkle. If it's time to have a bowel movement, suggest the flowers need to be fertilized!
- **Sweeter than roses.** Tell your child how nice she smells now that she's used the potty and kept her pants clean. To drive home the message, squirt her with a dollop of cologne. Little boys love this, too.

34

- **Toilet rainbows.** Add a few drops of blue food coloring in the toilet bowl (or a bit of water and food coloring to potty bowl) so your child can delight in watching it turn green when he adds yellow urine. Or color the water red so she can turn it orange.
- **Move it!** Nowhere is it written that a child must go to the potty. The potty can just as easily go to your child. Suggest he move it into the play area, put it in his bedroom at night, set it in the kitchen during meals. Try a pet pad under the potty seat in a carpeted room. It helps soak up spills and splashes.

Accident Prevention

Whether they are occasional or constant, accidents really are exactly that—accidents. They don't mean that your little one is purposely trying to upset you. Rather, the struggle is unconscious. Often children avoid all thoughts about the potty because it is a source of tension, parental anger, and personal defeat. Instead, remember that the best tricks for avoiding accidents are the games that make the potty so much fun, your child won't be able to resist using it!

The most effective solution for parents is to handle accidents calmly. Most important, avoid reproaching your child. That way, if you are convinced she is wetting and soiling "just to get you," she will soon lose her motivation to wet and soil if you don't get upset. You can, however, insist that she participate by changing her clothes and helping with cleanup.

Make Her a Cleanup Assistant

By age three, children should be able to participate actively in cleaning up accidents. It may be difficult not to be angry, but it is very important that you aren't. Your role is to teach, and there are merits to teaching them responsibility and how to help clean up. Show your child how to put the dirty clothes in the hamper. After the clothes are washed, he can work on her colors and shapes and sizes while learning to match socks (great for cognitive development) while you fold and separate. Then, help her put the clothes away in drawers she can reach so she can change herself with as little help as possible.

Help Her Remember to Go

If you have tried everything you can think of and your child keeps forgetting to go to the potty, perhaps having her go about bare-bottomed can help her remember. Turn up the thermostat, tell her not to have an accident, and remind her to use the potty when it looks like she might need to. Girls can go naked under a dress; it might work for a boy to wear pants without underwear.

When she is holding herself or looks like she needs to use the potty, ask if she wants to go to the potty or wants you to bring it to her. Sometimes offering a choice instead of telling toddlers what to do works better. If she declines both, tell her if she has an accident she will have to put away her toys until she helps clean up and changes her clothes. If she does have an accident, be true to your word!

Say, "Oops!"

Cheer up your little one by reassuring her that eventually she will remember to listen to her body when it announces that it is time for her urine to come out. Until then, accidents will happen. They are not the end of the world! Teach her to say, "Oops!"

Toilet Terrors

Any kind of frightening potty experience can cause your child to have a training setback. That could be falling off of the potty or thinking that he might, falling in the toilet or imagining that he could, having a bad dream about a potty, being startled by a shout or slap while on the potty, or hearing a loud noise while thinking about the potty. When you're a toddler, fantasy and reality blur all too easily, so it's easy to think that sharks live in the bowl and then believe it's true.

Fear of His Own Toilet

Here are some ways to help a child overcome a fear of a toilet or potty:

1. If the toilet is the issue, see if he will use a potty chair. If he had a scare on his potty chair, try switching to a potty seat.
2. Try dropping the word "potty" from your vocabulary. Maybe he needs to "visit Henrietta" and "sit on her lap," or see if Mrs. Tank is "hungry" or "needs a drink."

3. Do some decorating. Tie a ribbon or bow tie around the lid, make a face with masking tape on the lid, and affix stickers. If that does not help, stop all practice sessions for a month to give your child time to forget. Do not even mention the potty.

4. Show him the plumbing. If your child has seen Mr. Clean leap from the bowl on TV or has heard the day care rumor that tigers, dinosaurs, or spiders live in toilet water, open the tank so he can see what's inside (too small for a tiger, that's for sure). Demonstrate how to flush from inside the tank by lifting the lever, so that he can watch how the water rushes in through a tiny hole (too small for a tiger, that's for sure) then stops when the tank is full. Show him where the water leaves the toilet bowl through the little pipe in back (too small for a tiger, that's for sure).

5. Give him a magic wand or flashlight for protection. Explain that every time he waves the wand or shines the light around the toilet, the monster will weaken until it leaves or dies.

Fear of Public Toilets

Toilets in public restrooms can also be a real problem. The automatic kinds flush without warning. They are noisy, the water agitates violently, and the whoosh as the water is sucked away can be as loud as a vacuum cleaner, as if to warn him that he could be next. Carrying a portable potty that your child can use in the car may solve the problem until he's over a public restroom phobia.

38

 **Essential**

When you're out with a curious toddler, allow extra time so she can check out all the toilets in town. If you feel as though your outings are totally centered around the restrooms and your hands are tied, they probably are. Rest assured that this too shall pass. Don't decide he couldn't possibly need to use the toilet yet again—if he is nervous about whether or not you will take him when he needs to go, the likelihood of an accident increases. Also, teach your child to be respectful by not peeking under the stall to see what others are up to.

Encopresis

In the absence of a medical problem, a particular chain of events can lead to a lot of resistance or even full-blown encopresis—chronic constipation. It often begins when a child is slightly constipated, so the stool is a bit harder than normal; when it lands in the toilet bowl, the cold water splashes, hitting her bottom. The combination of surprise and discomfort makes the youngster nervous, even a bit afraid, of having a B.M. in the toilet again. She becomes tense and starts trying to hold in bowel movements to the point that she becomes even more constipated. When she does manage to have another bowel movement, the hard stools can be even more painful to pass.

A vicious cycle develops if a child is reluctant to pass stool for any reason, and she can become increasingly constipated. Bowel movements become increasingly hard and painful, which further adds to the child's reluctance to pass them. The situation can escalate to the point that a mass too large and hard to pass through the rectum forms in the bowel. Liquidy stool eventually passes around the mass and leaks out involuntarily and is often mistaken for diarrhea.

Treatment for Encopresis

First of all, call your pediatrician if you think your child may be experiencing signs of encopresis. To break the cycle, your doctor will probably recommend that you address the constipation, perhaps with a stool softener, extra fluids, and a high-fiber diet, that will, once it takes effect, prevent her from holding it in. Kids with encopresis typically need a "clean-out" regimen to get a lot of the stool out before a maintenance treatment plan of fiber and stool softeners will work. The "clean-out" regimen can include an enema or higher doses of stool softeners. While your child is being treated for encopresis, if bowel movements become too frequent or watery, the dosage of stool softeners can be reduced, but they often need to be continued for many months.

Create Positive Associations

Because children in this situation have come to associate the potty with physical pain and discomfort, breaking the negative associations and creating new, more positive ones may take a while and require a lot of help. Once her treatments take effect and the child has been having regular soft bowel movements each day, it is likely time to help your child have bowel movements while sitting on the potty again. Return to potty-learning strategies of rewarding and praising for small accomplishments.

Bedwetting

Even if your child uses the potty without fail during the day, he may still wet the bed. He may not awaken, or, if he does, may not feel like getting up. Instead of forcing him to get up, if he stays dry for several nights, try putting him to bed without a diaper to see if he is ready. If he's not, understand that many kids don't stay dry at night until they are closer to five years old.

He May Just Need to Outgrow It

Many children cannot awaken until they mature sufficiently, and punishing a child for this problem is abusive. If a child does wake up when his bladder is full, placing the potty near the bed can motivate him to use it. Instead of pressuring him, suggest he wear a diaper until he is ready to use the potty at night.

It can be hard to tell whether bedwetting stems from the I-don't-feel-like-getting-out-of-bed-to-use-the-potty-at-night syndrome, as most parents tend to think at first. Boys are more likely to be bedwetters, and since 15 percent of bedwetters spontaneously outgrow the problem every year, physical maturity is thought to be a factor. Most bedwetters have relatives who had the same problem as children, so heredity is also thought to play a role.

Physical Causes

Physical problems ranging from small bladder size to a bladder infection can cause incontinence. However, they are thought to affect less than 3 percent of children. Many can be easily corrected. Sleep apnea can prevent children from awakening so they can use the potty; the brain never receives the bladder's signal that it is full. Eventually the sphincter gives way, causing an accident. If apnea is due to problems with the adenoids and tonsils, it can be surgically treated. Apnea is sometimes difficult to diagnose because obvious symptoms, including loud snoring and pauses in your child's breathing, may only be present at night, so children can appear healthy when examined by a doctor.

Bedwetting also can infrequently be the result of bladder infection, a hormone deficiency, petit mal seizures, diabetes, a small bladder, a physical abnormality or malformation, or a central nervous system disorder.

Deep Sleep

The usual problem that causes millions of youngsters to wet the bed is that they sleep so deeply, they simply don't awaken so they can use the potty. They may have some dry nights, but if they can't manage to go a full month without wetting the bed, the diagnosis may turn out to be "primary enuresis." What keeps them from awakening isn't understood.

Children who stay dry every night for a month and then start wetting the bed again probably have "secondary enuresis." The usual causes are fatigue, stress, and depression, all of which cause children to sleep more soundly than usual. Like youngsters suffering from primary enuresis, they are unable to wake up. The problem can be expected to disappear as soon as the child is back on an even keel.

 Alert

Chlorine bleach and regular laundry detergents don't kill the bacterial spores that grow in urine, so the odor will reappear after linens and clothes have been washed. Try first soaking them in an enzyme bleach or borax solution. Better yet, keep your preschooler or younger school-age child in a nighttime pull-up or use a plastic sheet protector so that you aren't washing his bedding every day.

Problem-Solving

If your child is five years old and is still wetting the bed, your pediatrician will likely do a full medical exam (to rule out organic problems), a brief psychological exam (to rule out changes in the child's life that could cause increased exhaustion or stress), and a thorough family history (to investigate the possibility of an inherited problem). Since secondary enuresis can be caused by stress and other medical conditions, and since punishing children causes them to feel more stressed, it is important that you not overreact to your child's bedwetting. Otherwise, you could inadvertently make the situation worse. Remember that bedwetting is usually considered to be completely normal before age five and often isn't treated until kids are about seven or eight years old.

SHOULD WE RESTRICT FLUIDS?

Eliminate liquids that irritate the bladder and increase the frequency of urination (such as caffeine) and do avoid *lots* of fluids late in the evening, but know that normal fluid intake does not cause bedwetting. Good hydration is necessary for your child's health. When children are dehydrated their urine is more concentrated, which only increases urinary urgency.

 **Question**

Are there any reputable programs to help with bed-wetting?
If your child wets the bed because of a chronic inability to awaken, be careful of the many outrageously overpriced treatment programs from companies with questionable reputations that prey on desperate parents. One safe option is Try-for-Dry. It offers a free self-guided diagnosis and treatment program at *www .tryfordry.com* so that parents need only purchase the materials they need.

DETERMINE PATTERNS

Keep track of wetting incidents for a week. Once you've established your child's patterns, awaken him ten to twenty minutes before he is likely to wet the bed and take him to the bathroom to see if he can use it. Even if he never fully awakens, you may be able to avoid some accidents. Moreover, if you can consistently head them off for several months, you may be able to cure the problem by conditioning him. Exactly how this conditioning works is not understood. Rather than learning to get up at night, most children who have been successfully conditioned simply sleep through the night and stay dry without ever using the potty. If wetting starts up again after they have been conditioned, parents may need to take them to the potty every night for a few days to provide their brain with a "tune-up."

You might also check your child to see if he is dry ten or fifteen minutes before he normally wakes up. Some kids actually stay dry all night and then urinate first thing in the morning, instead of getting out of bed to use the bathroom.

CONSIDERING MEDICATIONS AND "ALARMS"

Bedwetting specialists often recommend that parents of older children try to determine the time at which the accidents typically occur by conducting frequent underwear checks or outfitting children with a moisture-sensitive unit that activates an alarm when urination begins. When the unit's electrical pad is moistened, a bell rings or a buzzer sounds. In the past, these were very pricey items; now they are readily available through outlets that specialize in potty-training products. However, some parents complain that they either don't wake up the child or they wake up everyone in the house, which can be especially troublesome since they often have to be used for several months to be effective.

In addition, some medications can be helpful to bed-wetters, though they are not typically used with children younger than age six or seven. Talk to your pediatrician if you feel your child may benefit from using an alarm or medicine. Bedwetting medications, like DDAVP, can be especially helpful when used on an as-needed basis for older kids when they start having sleepovers or going on campouts, etc. They aren't cures, though, and kids typically start wetting again when you stop the medication.

Be Understanding

Above all, be kind to your bedwetter! In an effort to protect themselves from continuing blows to their self-esteem, some youngsters adopt an I-could-care-less attitude. Parents may mistakenly conclude that they are not motivated to solve the problem or worse—are purposely wetting the bed—and react by becoming increasingly punitive. Since stress and depression cause secondary enuresis, parental negativity, shaming, and harsh punishments can cause what might have been a passing problem to become entrenched. Instead, provide sympathy and reassurance that your child is still too young to awaken at night.

CHAPTER 3

Bedtime

Just as toddlers need to tune in to the internal signals that let them know when and how much they need to eat, it is essential that toddlers learn to interpret the internal cues that indicate a need for sleep so that one day they can take care of themselves. Here's how to help them do that.

How Much Sleep Do Toddlers Need?

How can parents decide how much sleep their toddler needs? If a child is relaxed and content, it's doubtful that she's sleep deprived, even if you have deep circles under your eyes from entertaining her eighteen hours a day. But since fussier toddlers tend to have more difficulties sleeping, it can be hard to sort out whether the fussiness is caused by a lack of sleep or if their high-strung personality keeps them from getting concentrated, restful sleep.

Naps, of course, contribute to a toddler's overall sleep total. The journal *Sleep* reported that nine- to twelve-month-olds averaged two naps per day. At fifteen to twenty-five months, the average dropped to one afternoon nap. Most children continue afternoon naps until age four or five.

Cribs

The next question after "How much should my child sleep?" is often "Where should she sleep?" Depending on your child's age and preferences, you may be using or considering a crib, toddler bed, or family bed.

If you're using or considering a crib, above all, be sure you have one that's safe. Some cribs are recalled due to safety defects and hazards, so check with the manufacturer before making your purchase. When conducting your own inspection, watch for the three common problems. First, the slats should be strong and there shouldn't be any missing, broken, or loose hardware, including screws and brackets. Second, make sure the mattress fits well in the crib. Third, make sure the side rail does not slide down. The U.S. Consumer Product Safety Commission outlawed drop-side cribs in 2010. If you are buying a new crib, it will meet the latest safety standards, including having slats that are no more than $2\frac{3}{8}$ inches apart and having no lead paint. You should also avoid cribs with corner posts more than $\frac{1}{16}$ inch high and headboard or footboard cutouts (baby's clothing could get caught).

Have a Climber?

Cribs are not for climbers! Be careful about putting toys into a toddler's crib; if she steps on top of them, it may give her just the boost she needs to make it up the side and over the bars. A fall from such a great height poses the risk of injury. Some toddlers surprise their parents by managing to climb out not long after their first birthdays. Move the mattress to its lowest setting and remove crib bumpers if you have them so your toddler can't climb out easily. As soon as your little one begins scaling the bars, it's time to move to a toddler bed, though. You might make the move once your toddler is 36 inches tall, even if she hasn't tried to climb out yet.

Toddler Beds

Toddler beds are a great next step because they have raised sides to keep youngsters from falling out—and from feeling afraid they might fall out. They are also closer to the floor and pose less danger in case a child finds it fun to climb over the side. They aren't a magic solution to your toddler's sleeping problems, so don't make the move just because your toddler is not sleeping well in a crib.

 Alert

> Many children are in love with their toddler bed initially because they're so easy to climb out of! If this becomes a problem, consider having the child sleep on the mattress on the floor.

Since many toddler beds use the same size mattress as a crib, it's best to stick with the old crib mattress if at all possible. The familiar feel and smell of the old mattress can help smooth the transition from the crib. The quality of toddler bed frames varies dramatically from brand to brand. If you plan to lie down with your child to read stories or sleep, be sure to get a model sturdy enough to support both of you.

Making the Transition

How will your toddler handle the transition from crib to toddler bed? There's simply no way to predict it. It's smooth for some, decidedly difficult for others. If a child is very resistant to change, slow to adapt to new situations, or a sentimentalist, leaving the safety and security of the crib can be trying. Given a toddler's love of predictability and routine, it's a bad idea to let him step into his room to find his beloved crib gone. He may not find his parent's idea of a great surprise to be so wonderful. Even if he didn't like his crib at all, it was the steady friend that kept him safe night after night for as long as he can remember.

 **Essential**

Difficulty with the transition to a strange bed is understandable. (Many adults have a hard time sleeping when they're away from home!) As with anything you are trying to teach your toddler, bedtime procedures are established with baby steps. Be patient and consistent.

Instead, if possible, provide a gradual transition. The secret to getting youngsters to give up their cribs more willingly, many parents say, is to have them participate in the process from the very beginning.

Staying Put

The toddler who won't stay put in a toddler bed poses a real dilemma for parents: What to do with a little one who scurries out of bed the minute parents have finished tucking him in? What to do with the little insomniac who rises in the middle of the night and forays into the living room when everyone is asleep? The first step to getting a child to stay in bed is to discuss it.

Explain that it is dangerous for him to be up by himself, that he must stay in bed unless it's an emergency, and that he is to call Mommy or Daddy from his bedroom if he needs something. After that explanation, which a child may or may not understand, make it a policy to studiously avoid further conversation during these situations. Limit verbal exchanges to repeating in a firm tone of voice, "You're supposed to stay in bed unless it's an emergency. Go back to bed and call if you need something." (This assumes the parent has a baby monitor or is close enough to his room to hear him call.)

Walk him back to his room, help him into bed, issue another reminder to call if he needs something, and leave. Toddlers in this situation are apt to cry or call before you make it through the bedroom door. If that happens, turn around and go right back to his bedside to check on him, just as you promised.

 Fact

It may seem inhumane to install a door protector and close the door to contain a toddler who keeps popping out of a toddler bed after everyone else is asleep. But given the danger youngsters can get into roaming the house, it may be the only recourse. Be sure to *completely* childproof the bedroom first!

In getting across any new idea to a toddler, you need to take one step at a time and show him how things are supposed to go. Stepping out of the room and turning right back around to go back in demonstrates what is to happen: He calls; you respond. That can provide reassurance that having to be a big boy sleeping in a big bed doesn't mean he is expected to be independent. If a toddler doesn't start climbing back out of bed the moment you turn to leave, consider it a victory.

Remain calm and matter-of-fact as you approach your child's bed, and say, "I heard you calling. Is everything all right? What do you want?" Provide a drink of water if a child says he's thirsty; do the monster check again if he's scared; then give him a pat and tell him he's doing fine, that it will take a while to get used to the new bed. Repeat the procedure several times (but don't get in the habit of getting your child a drink every time), trying to avoid all conversation except:

- I heard you call. What do you want?
- You're fine now. It's time to get some sleep.
- Goodnight.

Begin extending the time between visits to the child's room.

The Family Bed

Another sleep location for a toddler is a family bed, where some members (or the entire family) sleep together. American taboos are quickly falling by the wayside as more parents find that the age-old solution of letting toddlers sleep with them virtually eliminates bedtime scenes and helps everyone rest better. Although this practice appears more kid-friendly on the surface, however, there's no guarantee that it will enhance a toddler's life. The loss of the parent's alone time can make it harder to remain patient with the youngster during the day, which is clearly not in a toddler's best interest. Additionally, the loss of private time with the spouse can jeopardize marital relationships, which, given the stress of rearing a toddler, may already be strained. Some parents also find that they have to go to bed at the same time as their toddler once they start to sleep in the same bed. Still, co-sleeping does seem to work for many families.

Big Bed Safety

Although crib safety gets a lot of attention, it is important to keep in mind that kids can get hurt in toddler beds too. To reduce these injuries, make sure the upper edge of the guardrail is at least 5 inches above the mattress, the beds slats are strong, and you heed warning labels about entrapment and strangulation hazards. Accidents also occur in big beds, and parents should take commonsense precautions before deciding to sleep with their little one. This includes making sure your child can't get trapped between the bed and the wall or headboard, etc., that she can't fall off the bed, and that you don't put her to sleep on a waterbed or one with soft bedding. Also, be sure that you don't roll onto your younger child.

Bad Bedfellow?

Many parents find that having the family snuggled up together in the same bed produces some of their warmest moments. Others find it far from pleasant. Some toddlers thrash, toss, elbow, wiggle, wet, and generally make difficult sleeping companions. Early risers may chatter, hum, poke, and play.

If parents don't want to share their bed, moving the crib or toddler bed into the parents' bedroom can eliminate the loneliness and enhance children's sense of safety and security. This can sometimes translate into less resistance at bedtime. Some children can tolerate being on the opposite side of the room with a curtain or room divider to provide some privacy for the parents.

If parents decide to move a small bedfellow, the best time to initiate the project is when separation and attachment issues may be less of a factor—typically around age three. Otherwise, aim for a period when the child isn't going through a lot of other difficult adjustments, separation anxiety isn't a major issue, the child wants to grow up rather than regress to baby days, and independence conflicts aren't paramount.

Sleep Schedules

Having a toddler on a sane sleep schedule makes for a calmer household, but it may take some time and cooperation among all the family members. Whether you and your toddler are both up frequently working on the Ferber method (see "Managing the Transition" later in this chapter) or you let him stay up until he collapses from exhaustion, it works best to get him up at the same time each morning and prevent long naps that compensate for missed sleep. Studies on insomnia demonstrate that establishing a schedule is helpful. Being extra-tired ups the odds that children will be ready to sleep at the next nap or bedtime.

The invariable routine of a set bedtime and nap schedule goes a long way toward regulating toddlers' sleep patterns. The human body operates in circadian rhythms—a predictable cycle that causes people to fall asleep at night and awaken in the morning at about the same time each day. These rhythms change over the life span. If left to their own devices, teenagers would stay up half the night and sleep half the day; on the other hand, senior citizens naturally fall asleep early and awaken shortly after dawn. In general, toddlers will be happier with themselves if sleep is regular and orderly.

Nighttime Rituals to Help Wind Down

A common reason that children of all ages don't want to sleep is that they don't want to miss out on something. They want to live every moment to the fullest. They don't want to be shut up alone in a room while other family members are out in the living room having fun. Even if everyone else is in bed, some youngsters would rather be out in the living room having fun all by themselves than lying awake in a darkened room. To avoid this, create rituals that ensure the toddler is sleepy when she goes into her bed.

Insisting that toddlers nap or go to bed when they *aren't* sleepy can provoke power struggles. Instead, have them observe quiet time. To create a quiet and relaxing transition, help them unwind by providing soothing entertainment such as listening to music or looking at books. Bath routines help, too. Rituals should be designed to soothe, so avoid stimulating activities like roughhousing, tickling, and exciting or scary stories.

 Alert

Nursing and giving children a bottle to help them fall asleep is not a good idea, dentists say, because the milk pools in their mouths, rotting their teeth. The same problem applies to juice and other sweet beverages. Remember: only water if you must give a drink!

To facilitate getting a toddler to sleep, try getting her into bed when she's sleepy but not overtired. This means she's physically more relaxed. It's harder when she's physically and emotionally tense from being overtired. Once they do relax, sleep may not be far behind. Even if sleep doesn't follow immediately, children need to learn to relax and spend time entertaining themselves. If you're still struggling to help your little one calm down, try one of these common strategies:

- Rock her.
- Sing lullabies.
- Tell a soothing story.
- Give her a back rub.
- Hold her hand.

These kinds of rituals induce relaxation and can help toddlers make the transition from a busy, active day to sleep. Going through an invariable progression from taking a bath, hearing a story, listening to a lullaby, and saying prayers helps toddler insomniacs, just like their adult counterparts. As people come to associate the ritual with sleep, their bodies automatically begin to relax.

 **Essential**

A noisy environment can certainly interfere with a child's ability to fall or stay asleep. After entering dreamland, some can tolerate a lot of hullabaloo; others remain susceptible to being awakened by sounds, especially during lighter phases of sleep. If you can't produce a quiet environment on cue, soft white noise can help mask telltale sounds that suggest interesting happenings are going on elsewhere in the house.

Letting toddlers be in charge of some bedtime decisions can help satisfy their need to be in control. Let them pick which story is read, which pajamas are worn, which stuffed animals go into the crib or bed, whether the nightlight is on or off, and which song you sing.

Sleep Skills

Though parent-led nighttime rituals are certainly an important component of getting a child to sleep, it's equally important to emphasize child-led soothing techniques. The downside of all that parental rocking, singing, and back rubbing to quiet a fretful child and help him fall asleep is that he comes to depend on someone or something outside of himself—a real problem if he wakes up in the middle of the night. Children need to learn eventually to handle the task of falling asleep—and of falling *back* asleep—unassisted. Surprisingly, the skills needed to do that don't come naturally to many children.

 Alert

> Some children engage in rituals such as repetitive rocking, which can escalate into head banging, as a way to soothe themselves. It usually stops by eighteen months. You can help by not overreacting, talking to your pediatrician to reassure yourself that it is normal, and by beefing up other bedtime rituals to provide a more gradual transition.

The first step is for children to learn to spend time alone. Being comfortable spending time alone in a crib or toddler bed is a prerequisite for falling asleep and for falling back asleep. By handing toddlers a stuffed animal after they awaken in the morning or from a nap, leaving the room, and waiting five to fifteen minutes to "rescue" them, parents can give them time to practice being by themselves. Some experts say this can serve them well at night.

Another technique is to put the child into his crib or bed before he falls asleep, so he grows used to being in the crib and falling asleep on his own. "On his own" doesn't mean totally without help, however. You can leave a pacifier in the crib within his reach (or even offer it to him to suck) if he is used to having it. You can also leave toddlers a cuddly, small stuffed animal in the corner of the crib or a small, lightweight blanket. A night-light can help toddlers see that there's nothing fearsome lurking.

If you do need to tend to a child who wakes up in the middle of the night, keep the room darkened or the light subdued, keep ambient noise hushed (which means this isn't the time to turn on music to soothe him), keep your voice low, and don't play games with him. You want to signal him that it's sleep time, not awake time.

Holding Firm

If you decide to start insisting that a child put herself to sleep (or back to sleep) on her own, it will likely be an exhausting and frustrating (but worthwhile!) venture. When a toddler's negativity sets in and she feels driven to disagree with every other thing the parent does or says, she may resist going to bed just because she's been told that's what she must do. Again, parents need to resist taking this personally and remain focused on the child's innate struggle for autonomy and independence.

In two-parent homes, it may be best to have the adult who is less intensely connected to the child be the one to manage bedtime complaints and middle-of-the-night pleas for attention. Since bedtime brings up separation issues for adults as well as for children, the more connected parent may experience some anxiety that the child picks up on. This can intensify the distress and separation anxiety of both. The parent in charge of putting the child to bed should be firm and matter-of-fact.

Handling Hysteria

Some toddlers will intensely resist such a change in routine. What happens when parents refrain from running into their wailing toddler's bedroom to help him fall asleep, and he is so upset he vomits? Or he cries so hard, he can't catch his breath and begins gasping for air? This is the point at which many parents decide the "he needs to learn to settle himself down" approach is doing more harm than good. Check with your pediatrician to see whether it's okay to hold firm under these circumstances. If so, be as sympathetic as you would toward any little person who is having such a hard time mastering something difficult. Then change the sheets, clean him up, tuck him in, give him a pat, and tell him he'll be okay. Tell him it's time to sleep, wish him sweet dreams, and leave. Return a few minutes later to check on him to be sure he's not ill.

Managing the Transition

If a child awakens crying and you determine that he isn't ill, verbally reassure him that he is fine or offer a stuffed animal or other favored toy for comfort. What happens next is up to you. Experts' philosophies of what's best for toddlers differ. Sleep problems often seem like the toughest parenting issues to deal with, but they can be fixed, just like other issues. The key is to understand that methods that are acceptable to some parents may not work for others. To help your child sleep all night you can:

- Use the Ferber method, wherein you leave your child, even if he is crying, for progressively longer periods of time, before briefly checking on him again.

- Remain physically present to provide some reassurance and moral support while your child cries, moving a chair a few inches farther from the crib or bed each night until you are out the door, thereby helping the child to feel more secure while he learns to fall asleep on his own.

- Hold, rock, sing, carry, and otherwise soothe the child to help him fall asleep whenever he cries—the no-cry method.

- Invite the child into your bed.

Whether you sleep together or apart, or whether you respond to each call from the bedroom, don't judge others negatively for doing it their way—and don't let them judge you.

Monsters and Nightmares

The brain waves of tiny babies suggest that even the youngest members of our species dream. Similarly, some toddlers have nightmares. Because children in this age group have such a poor ability to distinguish reality from fantasy, it can be impossible to convince them that the monsters and big bad bears aren't real. Nevertheless, provide lots of reassurance that "it was just a dream." When they're old enough, they'll understand the difference.

Monster Patrol

Ongoing worries about monsters and burglars among older children are sometimes rooted in nighttime fear and loneliness. If fears of the dark are keeping your toddler awake, try dousing monsters and assorted goblins in beams from a nightlight. Often a fear of a nighttime visit from a wild animal or cartoon character can be overcome by outfitting the child with a "special repellent" guaranteed to render a beastie harmless. The repellant can be anything from a flashlight to a designated stick they can wave like a magic wand to some special pajamas. Since sound can banish monsters, keeping a rattle under their pillow to shake at the shadows in their closet and the branches outside their window can also hold imaginary beasts at bay. Placing a protective object in the room, such as an oversized teddy bear to stand watch, can be reassuring.

 Fact

Some toddlers are affected more than others, but anything containing caffeine is on the list of before bedtime no-nos—exactly how long before depends on the toddler. Likewise, it's a good idea to keep anything with caffeine off the list of toddler foods and beverages, especially if getting them down for naps is a problem. Some people also think that cane sugar and artificial colorings can affect some kids' sleep and behavior patterns.

There are no proven ways to eliminate nightmares, but you can encourage your child to share the bad dreams, since this may help her feel better. If her vocabulary is limited, try to help her tell it. If she says, "Bear," ask, "Was it a scary bear?" Avoid questions like, "Was the bear trying to eat somebody?" so as not to implant more fear!

Night Terrors

These sudden, unexplained bouts of screaming and wild thrashing within the first few hours of going to sleep can be terrifying to parents who find themselves unable to comfort their youngster. Although a child appears to be awake, she may actually be asleep during these episodes and have no memory of them on awakening. Night terrors are believed to occur at the transition from one phase of sleep to another. They are more common when kids are overtired, and many kids eventually outgrow having night terrors when they get older.

CHAPTER 4

Teaching Discipline

Ultimately, the goal of teaching rules and discipline is for your toddler to learn to control herself instead of relying on adults to control her. But developing self-control won't be accomplished in a matter of days, weeks, or even months or years. Until then, you may be better off putting more energy into controlling the environment. That way, you can spend less time struggling to control your youngsters and more time enjoying them.

Little Learners

Teaching toddlers rules and self-control is a long, slow process. They have little experience on which to build, and their language skills prevent them from telling you they understand much of what is said to them. In addition, their attention level and memory skills are not very well developed, so that they forget much of what they've been taught from moment to moment and from day to day. Finally, they lack the intellectual skills to always know to use what they learn in one situation to guide their behavior in another.

The solution to many problems becomes obvious once parents understand what is driving toddlers to act as they do. Don't assume that troublesome behavior stems from naughtiness, contrariness, or mindless negativity. Look at what toddlers are trying to achieve. Be flexible as you help them achieve their goals in an acceptable manner. Most toddlers are just exploring their environment and seeing what they can get away with, and aren't trying to be defiant.

Teaching about *No*

When you say "no," it may be clear in your mind exactly what you want the toddler to stop doing or to stay away from. But what is obvious to you may not be at all clear to the toddler.

How do you teach what *no* means? Here are a few ideas:

- Change your tone of voice when you say it. Use a firm, low tone of voice, and maintain direct eye contact.
- Accompany your words with a frown and shake of the head.
- Use a gesture and point at what you are talking about.
- Offer positive reinforcement when your child listens well.

Toddlers may still not associate the phrase and gesture with an expected behavior, but at least they are being helped to focus on that important word.

Don't *Just* Say "No"

The problem with just saying "no" is that toddlers don't learn what they can do. A child may not be trying to create chaos and ill will as she goes from one forbidden activity to the next. She doesn't know what is off limits and what is permissible. And unfortunately, if your toddler hears "no" too often, especially without a clear consequence to follow up, she will learn to tune you out. Instead of so many "nos" try redirecting your child to another behavior or activity. Offering alternatives may not prevent toddlers from becoming upset if they're very involved with something, but offering alternatives provides an important lesson: When the road she wants to go down is blocked, she needs to find another road.

The easiest way for parents to reduce the number of "no-nos" and "don't touches" is to childproof the home by putting away and securing as many dangerous and fragile objects as possible, and to provide lots of objects for your toddler to use and enjoy. This gives your child an environment to learn, play, and explore without getting in trouble all the time.

"No" Can Be Confusing

As anyone who has studied a foreign language knows, learning to understand and use negative words is no small task. In English, things get particularly confusing. Even adults aren't always sure what answering "yes" to a question means; for example, "You're not going to touch the stove, are you?" When addressing toddlers, keep things very direct and simple!

Since negatives like "don't" occur at the beginning of sentences, toddlers often don't hear them. Especially in a noisy environment, they may not even realize they're being spoken to until you have made it halfway through the sentence. So when you say, "Don't touch the stove," the toddler may only hear ". . . touch the stove" or ". . . the stove." It's no wonder toddlers sometimes do exactly the opposite of what their parents are telling them! This is not willful disobedience. They are struggling to attend to what they've heard.

You can also try telling your toddler what to do rather than what not to do. Instead of "Don't touch the stove," you might say instead, "Keep your hands at your sides!" or "Come over here right now." Or add a simple explanation so that they know why you do or don't want them to do something, like "Don't touch the stove because it will burn your hand."

Discipline Is Not Punishment

Many people think of discipline as punishment, and this is unfortunate. Literally, discipline means to teach or to learn. Disciplining toddlers involves helping them learn how to behave so that they become comfortable in their lives and in the company of other people. Parents are the most important teachers in this goal.

 Fact

Setting limits and boundaries on your child's behavior does not mean taking away his freedom or autonomy. You can still allow your child to have many choices within the parameters that you set. For example, "Playing ball in the street is not safe. You can play in the backyard. Would you rather play soccer or baseball?"

Ultimately, you want your child to attain self-discipline, and during the toddler years, you start to build a foundation for inner self-control. The more self-control your child has, the less likely he will be to have temper tantrums (more on that in the next chapter). Self-control allows your child to regulate and control his emotions. Learning self-control is an ongoing process that occurs with your support and discipline. Your child needs limits and external boundaries in order for him to internalize rules and standards of behavior that will allow him to develop self-control. He needs to know that an adult is there to guide him and keep him safe and in control. When he is feeling confused, scared, frustrated, angry, or overwhelmed, he will count on you to guide him with authority and control.

If you choose to set very few or no limitations on your child's behavior, he will have a difficult time learning safe, appropriate behavior and self-control. You are handing over to your child the control to regulate his own behavior. This parenting style or approach is known as permissive parenting. Permissive parents will usually establish very few rules and often do not consistently enforce the rules that they have set. Due to your child's lack of experience, and his cognitive and emotional immaturity, this approach may not be effective. If and when your child fails at regulating his own behavior, he could be more likely to have outbursts and temper tantrums and to lose his self-control.

How to Set Limits

By establishing rules, you are setting limits and parameters for your child's safe and acceptable behavior. These rules should clearly communicate your expectations. When your child is very young, you will take sole responsibility for establishing all rules and codes of conduct. Once your child is past three years old, you should consider involving her when you are generating the rules. There are many benefits to involving your child. If she is

70

involved in a discussion about potential rules, she will be more likely to understand their importance. She will be more likely to comply with rules she thought of and agreed with. Additionally, she will be less likely to view rules as arbitrary or unfair.

 Alert

> Toddlers can be very literal and rigid when they hear and interpret rules. When you say, "Food stays in the kitchen," your toddler may insist that Spike's food bowls be brought up from the garage. Additionally, your young toddler may overgeneralize a rule. For example, when you allow her to use soap paint on the bathtub walls, she may think painting on any walls with any type of paint is okay.

Although you want your expectations to be clear, it is neither wise nor practical to list a rule for every possible infraction. First, you will never be able to anticipate all of your child's future misbehaviors. Second, you will end up with a list of rules more lengthy and complex than the federal tax code. Consider your priorities. Pick just a few clear and easy-to-remember rules that you feel will serve as guidelines in helping your child learn safe behavior and self-control. Consider your child's developmental abilities. Make sure the rules reflect reasonable expectations for her age and maturity. For children under school age, three to five rules are optimal. Even for older children, keep the lists short; after all, there are only ten commandments.

Keep Your Expectations Clear

The rules should be a clear statement of your expectations for your child's behavior. Rules should be brief and to the point. Avoid rules that include exceptions and variable factors. Here is an example of such a rule that you shouldn't use: "Don't play with your red ball in the dining room or kitchen, and don't play with it in the living room if we have guests visiting (unless I say it's okay)." Not only is this rule confusing, but it is nearly impossible for your small child to remember all the details.

Keep Your Expectations Specific

Do not expect your child to be a mind reader. State your expectations very specifically and remind your kids about them. Parents often just tell children directives such as "be nice," "be good for Grandma," and "don't act up!" Remember that your standards or ideals of what is "well behaved" will probably be vastly different from what your child considers "well behaved." When you tell your five-year-old that you want his room to be clean, you are envisioning a room where all of the books are lined up in alphabetical order, the bed is made with fresh sheets, and his floor is mopped and waxed. Conversely, your five-year-old believes a clean room to be a room where all of the mess is hidden under the bed. Other examples of vague rule statements include "calm down" and "help out."

State Rules Positively

Rules should state what behavior you expect. Tell your child what to do. Avoid negatively phrased rules. Younger children, in particular, will focus on the action and disregard the negation. For example, when you tell your preschooler, "Do not go near the swimming pool without an adult," he focuses on the phrase "go near the swimming pool." "Stop pulling the cat's tail" becomes "pull the cat's tail." You can change a rule from negative to positive just by changing a few words.

CHANGING NEGATIVE RULES	
Negative Rules	**Become Positive Rules**
No running in the house.	Walk while you are in the house.
You may not eat in the living room.	Food stays in the kitchen.
Candy before dinner is not allowed.	Candy is allowed only after dinner.
No watching TV before your homework is done.	Do your homework before you watch TV.

If you look at the negative rules above, you can see how ambiguous they can be, especially to a child who is testing limits. When you say, "No running in the house," your child may ask, "What about galloping, sprinting, or spinning?" When you say, "You may not eat in the living room," they may ask, "What about my bedroom?" Notice how the positive rules are clear and defined, leaving less room for questioning.

Three Basic Rules to Start With

To keep expectations simple, you can set a few broad rules that can encompass your expectations of your child's behavior. Here are three suggested rules. You will find they are clear, are easy to remember, and will cover just about any misbehavior you would want to respond to.

1. **Be Safe to Others:** "Others" can include friends, family member, pets, and so forth. Unsafe behaviors include hitting, biting, grabbing, and teasing or name-calling (which "hurts" feelings). You may wish to explain to your child that you will not allow anyone to hurt him and you will not allow him to hurt others. You will also refer to the rule if he is hurting you.
2. **Be Safe to Yourself:** You can remind your child that it is important to you that he stay safe and healthy. This rule includes all behaviors that are unsafe to the child (running with scissors, playing in the busy street) and can also include behaviors that protect his health (hand washing, eating nutritious foods).
3. **Be Safe to Things:** You are asking your child to respect all toys, materials, and property. Behaviors that are not permissible as a result of this rule include breaking toys and coloring on walls.

Enforcing Rules and Limits

How you respond to misbehavior and how you enforce the limits you create will send strong messages to your child. You are showing her what behavior you expect and value. You are showing her that she can depend on you to help her regain and maintain control when she is acting out or having a temper tantrum.

Determine Your Priorities

For the sake of your own sanity, pick your battles and do not sweat the small stuff. Perhaps you want your child to eat nutritious food at every meal. Dinnertime rolls around and you become locked in a battle with your child. You are planning to serve peas but she wants asparagus instead. In the grand scheme of things, will it really matter if she has asparagus instead of peas? In fact, if your ultimate motivation is her health, a few meals without a vegetable serving at all will do no harm. Do not let the original rules or intent get lost in a battle of wills.

 Fact

Behaviors that do no harm, directly or indirectly, are often best ignored. These behaviors include tattling, whining, pouting, and bathroom or silly talk. In fact, responding to these types of behaviors will usually increase their frequency.

State the Reason for the Rule

Always try to state the reason for a rule as you enforce it. Your explanation does not need to be a lengthy lecture; a brief statement will do. For example, "Put your feet on the floor. It is not safe for you to climb on the railing. You could fall." "Return the scissors to their case so no one gets stabbed by them." When you state the reason for a rule, your child will be less likely to see the rule as arbitrary or as just your way of exerting power. Explanation statements such as "Because I am the dad" or "Because I said so" are statements that will surely be met with resistance by your child and do not teach anything.

Most important, when you repeatedly state the reason for a rule, you are helping your child learn the consequences of her actions, and you are promoting the development of her inner voice or conscience.

Finally, it is important to note that, if you are unable to explain or justify a rule, you should reconsider whether it is a fair or reasonable rule.

Consistent Enforcement

As your child is learning what it is that you expect from her, she is also learning what to expect from you. Consistently respond and enforce the limits and rules that you have set. Lax enforcement of your rules is no better than not having any rules at all.

For example, you have told your child that she may not play in the living room. The last few times you found her playing there, you removed the toys she was playing with and sent her to her room. However, on one occasion, you were in the middle of cooking dinner and it had been a hectic day for you. You decided to let this misbehavior slide, just once, promising yourself that you would be sure to punish her for both offenses the next time you saw her. The problem is, your child may interpret this by thinking she can get away with the misbehavior whenever you are busy or harried. Additionally, with rare exception, a rule should apply no matter where the child is, what time of day it is, or who is enforcing the rule. If not, your child will quickly learn that rules she can bend are the easiest rules to break.

 **Essential**

Empty threats are poisonous to both your child's behavior and your authority. It is wise and acceptable to tell your child the potential consequences of her actions: "If you throw those blocks one more time, I will put them away." However, it is critical that you follow through. If not, your child will quickly learn to disregard your threats in much the same way the village disregarded the boy who cried wolf.

And so, if Dad allows your child to stay up later than you do, there may be conflict. Your child may even learn to play one parent against the other. You will find that the most effective way to change and influence your child's behavior is to have all caregivers respond to and manage your child's behavior in a set and consistent fashion.

CHAPTER 5

Dealing with Tantrums

Tantrums are most common between ages two and three, when there can be as many as one or two daily. The toddler years are stereotypically known for tantrums, due in part to the fact that toddlers can be very opinionated. They have learned the true power of the word "no" and enjoy exercising their verbal prowess in no uncertain terms. For parents it can be exasperating.

Helping Preschoolers
Learn to Problem-Solve

Your efforts to help your child avoid tantrums begin with teaching him to problem-solve. Even infants and toddlers are beginning to learn how to solve problems. They are learning by direct hands-on exploration. Learning at this age comes from doing, by trial and error. Slowly, your child can see the consequences of his actions, such as learning how pushing a button on a toy makes a sound. This development will be helpful in your efforts to promote good behavior and avoid tantrums before they begin.

 Essential

Select toys that your child can explore and manipulate to see cause and effect. Some toys good for this are stacking rings, rattles, spinning toys, See 'n Say, or a jack-in-the-box. Toys that can be played with in more than one way, like boxes and blocks, are ideal.

As your child ages, his ability to master problem-solving will improve. Advancing verbal skills will aid his negotiation ability. Improved memory capacity will help him recall consequences of his behavior and will aid in learning through imitation. Now your child can try out multiple solutions and compare their effectiveness.

Role-playing is a great way to teach your child how to work through different alternatives to a tantrum. You can engage your preschooler's imagination by using dolls or puppets. Set up a scenario of interest with your child. Here are some suggestions for possible conflicts that can easily devolve into tantrums: Mr. Frog grabs the block away from Miss Spider, both Piglet and Pooh want the honey pot first, or the three bears find two apples in the forest. Be sure to include a discussion of each of the points of view and of the possible feelings of the characters. Remember to involve your child in generating possible solutions. Encourage your child to script the action. For example, you can ask him, "What can Miss Spider say to Mr. Frog so that she can get the block returned to her?"

Your school-aged child is starting to understand abstract thought. This frees him from trial-and-error learning. He does not have to physically try out multiple solutions; now he can imagine hypothetical situations and outcomes. Help your child develop these skills and learn to analyze and evaluate alternative solutions with the following activities:

- Use storybooks as a springboard for a discussion. Identify problems that characters are facing and evaluate how their problems are resolved.
- At the top of a large piece of butcher paper, list a potential problem or conflict the child has already experienced. Below, make two columns and title them "Good Choice" and "Bad Choice." Write potential reactions to the problem on index cards and have your child decide where each card belongs. Here is an example problem: You want the puppet that Jimmy is playing with. Here are example reactions: (a) You snatch the toy away from Jimmy, (b) You ask

Jimmy for a turn, (c) You find a new toy to play with until Jimmy is done, and (d) You bring a new puppet and ask Jimmy if he wishes to trade.

Preventing Tantrums

Temper tantrums are a normal part of your young child's behavior. Even while using clear limit-setting and proper enforcement, it is unrealistic to expect that you will be able to prevent all of them. You can, however, recognize some of the common triggers and causes of many of your child's temper tantrums. Once you can identify potential causes, you can prevent many tantrums before they happen.

Prevention is your first line of defense. You can prevent many problems simply by preparing in advance. Consider these ways to prevent many temper tantrums before they occur:

- **Be sure your child is well rested.** A tired child is more likely to become cranky. Most young children seem to fare better in the morning because they are more alert and not missing a needed naptime. Plan activities and errands accordingly.
- **Never go hungry.** A hungry child is more likely to lose emotional calm and balance, especially in stressful or tiring situations.
- **Dress your child appropriately.** Comfortable clothes and shoes are important. Try dressing your child in easy-to-remove layers to adjust to changes in tem-

perature. If your child is physically uncomfortable, it is likely that she will be cranky and more prone to having a tantrum.

General Strategies for Public Tantrums

Public places are unfortunately the site for many a toddler tantrum. Take heart, there are still steps you can take to reduce and manage these public meltdowns. The most important thing to remember is to stay calm. If you begin to raise your voice or become emotional, chances are your child's behavior will only escalate.

Prevent a Public Temper Tantrum

Again, prevention is your first line of defense. Here are some additional ideas that are helpful when you want to avoid tantrums when you're out and about:

- **Make a list.** When you have a child who is easily tempted and insists on having everything in the store he sees, try making a shopping list before the trip. Obtain a store flyer and encourage your child to choose one or two items in advance to be added to the list. Be sure to stick to this list in the store!
- **Review rules in advance.** Take time to review with the child what will be happening and how you will expect him to behave.
- **Patronize child-friendly stores.** Some stores have removed "high-temptation" items like candy and toys from the checkout area, or they have a candy-free

checkout aisle. Other stores have child-sized shopping carts, which help your child feel that he is participating and being a "big" helper, which ultimately prevents him from growing bored, tired, or cranky. While it may not be the magic charm every time, it is helpful in occupying his mind.

- **Choose off-peak times whenever possible.** Grocery stores are often the most chaotic in the early evening and on weekends. Tuesday mornings are ideal. On the other hand, doctor offices seem to be the quietest early in the morning and on Friday afternoons.

- **Engage and involve your child.** Even when the errand is not of interest to him, you can interact with him and keep his interest. Simply ask questions such as, "Who do you think could wear such teeny shoes?" or "How many people can you count in our line?"

- **Bring an emergency activity kit.** Bring a little backpack or tote with age-appropriate items for times when your child has to wait or may be restless or cranky. Depending on your child's interests, it may include sticker books, picture books, handheld games, and more. Keep this in your car so it is readily available. Be sure to rotate items to maintain interest.

When Trouble Is Brewing

Even if you've tried the prevention techniques, there are times that your child will still begin to struggle with errands or an outing. Here's what to do in those circumstances:

- **Respond promptly.** It may be easy to react with "just wait until we get home," but this does very little to help a child regain calm and composure. In addition, by the time you get home and address the issue, it is unlikely the child will be able to associate the original behavior with the delayed consequences.
- **Be flexible.** Be in tune with your child's moods and adjust your plans as needed. If you notice your child becoming fidgety in the shoe store, take a brief walk around the mall or stop for a pretzel before venturing on to the next store. Other early signs of trouble include increased crankiness and whining.
- **Offer a snack.** Even a small snack can boost your child's energy and mood. Keep a hidden stash of breadsticks or granola bars in your purse or glove compartment for a quick snack anytime.
- **Make concessions.** Not everything has to be an all-or-nothing battle. Sometimes offering a limited choice breaks the cycle of power struggles. For example, "Although I can't let you have every toy you see, you may choose one doll if you walk through the rest of the store nicely with me."
- **Avoid leaving.** Use the above strategies to help your child regain control. Do not simply give up on the errand or leave the location unless necessary. If you leave a location as soon as your child has a

tantrum, he will quickly learn to manipulate you to avoid going to unpleasant places such as the doctor's office.

- **Find a refuge.** When your child is having a full-fledged temper tantrum, take him to a quiet area away from the center of activity and traffic until you can help him calm down and regain control.

Maintain Consistency

Recognize that your child can learn to have more temper tantrums in public if you respond to a public temper tantrum differently than you do to one at home. If, to avoid embarrassment or conflict in public, you give in to your child's demands, he will quickly learn that his tantrums are more effective and worthwhile in public. It may be tempting to give in to your child's demands, to avoid the temper tantrum that is bound to follow. Stand your ground and make it clear that his tantrum is not going to get him what he wants.

 Fact

Many malls and larger stores now have supervised play or activity areas set up. Such a place may be very welcome for your bored or restless child and a needed break for you.

Studies show that, regardless of how parents respond to temper tantrums at home, many may respond to public temper tantrums with anger or embarrassment, which may cause parents to either harshly discipline their children or to give in to their demands.

Consistency is key. Respond to the temper tantrum in public in the same way that you would at home. If you ignore him at home, do the same at the store, even if this means pretending to read a cereal box. You may need to move your child to a quiet place, but in the long run, your child will learn there are set expectations for his behavior no matter where he is.

Strategies for Tantrums in Specific Places

Beyond the general guidelines, there are specific ways you can cope with your child's temper tantrums in a variety of settings. Each location or situation comes with its own set of potential challenges or problems that you may need to respond to. Public tantrums can, indeed, be particularly troublesome. However, as with tantrums at home, your calm and consistent response will result in diminishing displays of public temper tantrums.

Restaurants

Restaurants are a common setting for temper tantrums. You are probably asking your child to meet higher behavioral expectations than you would in the more informal home setting. Home may have a different set of rules. At home, you may allow her to leave the table when finished, or to get up and serve herself. In a restaurant, you ask your child to sit still, wait quietly, and exhibit her best manners, all while being hungry.

Look for restaurants that are child-friendly. Many restaurants now do several things to accommodate families with young children. Some restaurants provide puzzle place mats, tablecloths that can be colored, or even tabletop toys. Buffets can be ideal, and they have the added benefit of giving your child the chance to walk around a bit (with your supervision) and reduce her fidgetiness. When your child does have a temper tantrum, you will probably need to leave the table. Retreat to the restroom or lobby with your child. See Chapter 1 for more ideas on how to enjoy eating out.

Waiting Rooms

Doctor's offices and waiting rooms can be difficult places for a young child to remain calm and in control. Here again, you are asking your child to sit still and be quiet. Waiting rooms are notoriously uncomfortable places to be—the chairs are hard, the lights are harsh, and other people waiting may be uncomfortable or distraught. Unless you are in a pediatrician's office, it is unlikely there will be any toys, books, or pleasant distractions for your child. To make matters worse, your child may be ill or feeling anxious about the impending appointment. If your child has a meltdown, you may want to approach the receptionist. She may be able to delay your appointment until your child is calm. Conversely, if your child's temper tantrum is because of impatience, she may be able to arrange for you to be waited on sooner. It does not hurt to ask. Be sure to let her know if you are going to remove the child. Sometimes a brief stroll around the building will provide the distraction she needs.

Stores

A trip to the store can be challenging for a child. Shopping is simply not a fun activity for a young child. For what is usually an extended period, you are asking your child to either walk nicely by your side or to remain in a cart. They may see many attractive items that they find tempting but are not allowed to touch or have. Remember that stores are often hot, crowded, and noisy, adding to a child's irritability and yours as well.

 Essential

When your child is having a temper tantrum in public, find a refuge—a quiet area away from the center of activity and traffic. If you determine your child is having an attention-seeking tantrum, calmly tell him you will wait for him to stop before returning to the activity. If your child is having a tantrum for a developmental reason (frustration, poor verbal skills), patiently comfort her and address the issue at hand.

When Fun Places Are Not Fun

If your child has a temper tantrum at a fair, amusement park, or carnival, one of your first concerns needs to be safety. When your young child has a meltdown in one of these places, there is a risk that your child will run from you and be lost in the crowd or injured. Therefore, if your child is losing control, your first step is to contain her. Get her to sit down on a bench or lead her over to a pavilion.

If you determine that overexcitement and overstimulation are playing a part, find a place or activity for calming down. Many amusement parks offer more sedate activities that can be restful for both of you. Take a break from the wild rides and loud music and explore the surrounding gardens or the paddleboats on the lake. It is helpful to note that when your child has a temper tantrum in a "fun" place, leaving will not reinforce her tantrum and it may be an effective way to prevent further problems.

Visiting Other People

Before visiting other people's homes, be sure to define the rules clearly to your child. Inform her of any special restrictions in advance. Can she pet the dog? Are there off-limits items in the host's house? If your child has a temper tantrum, calmly excuse yourself and your child to the bathroom or porch and help your child regain control. If your child is unable to calm down, you may need to end the visit.

Fine Arts

If your child has a tantrum in a movie theater, everyone around you will know. More than likely, your child's tantrum will be a disruption to the other theatergoers. Recognize that your child may be more likely to act up if the movie content is scary or too mature for her. Immediately take your child to a quiet space such as the bathroom or the lobby to regain control. Allow your child time to settle down completely. Be sure she is ready to go back into the theater. If you suspect that the problem will continue, it may be best to leave. Young children often enjoy live theater more than movies. Many cities have a children's theater program geared toward young children. These productions are usually lively and interactive, which helps engage children and make them less likely to become upset.

Going for a Ride

Maybe the worst place for a temper tantrum is on mass transit. You and your child are taking an eight-hour bus ride or flight to visit Grandma. Your child's toy rolls under the seat and it is not retrievable. Predictably, your child goes into hysterics. There are very few places to take your child aside. Whether you are taking the crosstown bus or a transatlantic flight, be sure to bring some activities or books. It may help if you can get a seat by the window. If your child has a tantrum, you may need to find refuge in the bathroom or in the back row of seats. If you are truly stuck, you can try holding her or rubbing her back. One mother faced with this situation came up with a creative idea. She draped a travel blanket over them both. This gave them some privacy. It also helped the out-of-control toddler to focus on her mother's efforts to calm her down.

Helping Your Child Calm Himself Down

Having skills for self-soothing and self-calming is important—especially when children are dealing with the heightened emotional state of a tantrum. Children (and adults) who have these skills can handle stress and frustration better than those who don't. You can promote in your child the ability to maintain emotional equilibrium and the ability to roll with the punches.

Younger Children

Many young infants and toddlers adopt their own self-soothing behaviors. Thumb sucking may be the earliest example, but other children may rock gently, rub their face with a blanket or other loved object, or twirl their hair. There are many ways you can try to calm your child. Try some of the following to find which works best for him:

- Play soft music.
- Provide white or droning noise (such as a fan).
- Rock your child.
- Stroke or massage your child.

As your child approaches toddlerhood, there are some fun activities that you can use to show him how to calm himself down. Show him how to relax his body. Ask your child to let his muscles go limp and pretend to be a rag doll. Alternatively, ask him to swirl and twirl scarves in the air. Ask your young child to move like an animal: Stomp through mud like an elephant, fly and glide like a bird, and so forth. These activities force your child to slow down, relax, and move in a calm, controlled manner.

Activities that involve the sense of touch (kinesthetic activities) are often very soothing for young children. Use a bucket or dishpan for a sensory activity. Fill the bucket with water or sand or shaving cream or any tactile material your child may enjoy. Play-Doh, Gak, Silly Putty, and clay are also very calming materials for your child to manipulate.

Older Children

As your child matures, his ability to calm himself down will improve. Adults as well as children can use many of the activities below. Introduce your child to a variety of strategies and let him discover what works best for him.

- **Help your child find a special "get away from it all" place.** This can be a quiet room in the cellar, a grassy spot under an apple tree, or even just a comfy chair. Any place that he can call his own and where he will be undisturbed will work.
- **Provide opportunities for your child's self-expression.** A journal or sketchpad can sometimes help your child vent in a safe way. Provide him with any materials he may need, such as pencils, crayons, and so forth. Be sure to reassure your child that his journal is a private thing for him and that you will not look at it unless he invites you to.
- **Show your child ways to relax his body with these exercises.** Sit quietly, take deep breaths through your nose, and exhale slowly. Try imagining you are breathing through your feet. Listen to the sound of your breath. Curl your body into a tight ball. Slowly uncoil yourself like a cat stretching out. Be sure to

slowly stretch as far as you can go. Close your eyes.
Focus on one part of your body; clench it tightly.
Then relax that part slowly. Imagine it is very loose
and heavy. Work from your head to your toes.

- **Guide your child with creative visualization.** You can
read or tape scripts for your child to listen to. Here
are three to try.

  1. **Light as a Feather:** Close your eyes and relax.
     Imagine you are a light little feather. You are
     dropping slowly from a big white fluffy cloud in
     the sky. Feel yourself softly sway back and forth.
     Feel how the wind is pushing you as you glide
     downward. You are swaying back and forth, back
     and forth, and back and forth. Feel how a cool
     breeze makes you tumble through the air. You
     are slowly descending until you come to a gentle
     stop on the ground.

  2. **At the Beach:** You are lying on the warm sand at
     the beach. You can feel the cool and gritty sand
     under your back. You feel your feet sinking a bit
     in the moist sand. You now notice how warm
     the sun feels on your skin. When you turn your
     head, you can see all of the tiny crystals of sand,
     glimmering like diamonds in the sunlight. Take a
     deep breath; you can smell the warm, salty sea
     air and the lingering fragrance of suntan lotion.
     In the distance, you can hear children playing, a
     gull crying, and the waves crashing on the shore.

3. **In the Forest:** You are sitting underneath a great big tree in the middle of the forest. You are resting your back on the hard, rough, and knobby trunk of the tree. You can feel cool spongy moss under your hands as you rest them on the ground. At your feet is a babbling brook. The cool water is splashing up against the rocks and a refreshing spray is hitting your legs. The sunlight is streaming though the leaves and creating a dappled pattern on the forest floor. You close your eyes and you can hear the wind rustling through the leaves and the call of an unknown bird.

- **Try "writing" on your child's back like a blackboard.** Ask him to lie still on his stomach. Direct him to pay attention to what he feels. Use your finger to draw on your child's back. For younger children, make shapes and spirals. For the older child, you can draw specific shapes, letters, or numbers and ask him to guess what they are.
- **Make your child into a human burrito.** Tucking in your child like this can be part of a soothing ritual. Sometimes being firmly contained like this will calm an overwrought toddler. Spread a blanket out on top of your child's made bed. Have your child lie on top of the blanket on one side of the bed. Tuck the near side of the blanket over him and gently roll him across the bed until he is wrapped up in the blanket roll. Unroll your child before you leave him to rest quietly or go to sleep.

- **Sing!** Just about anything goes better when you are singing. Make up different verses to the tune of "Pop! Goes the Weasel." Potential verses might involve how to "dry our tears" and so on, adapted to whatever seems to be the child's difficulty. Here's an example:

This is the way we quiet down,

Quiet down, quiet down.

This is the way we quiet down,

So early in the morning.

It is often very difficult for young children to shift gears. They are unable to go from being active and wound-up to calm and restful without a transitional time. In other words, it is unrealistic to expect that your toddler will be able to go directly from a tantrum to a long and peaceful nap. Try to have a few routines with these calming activities in place to assist your child in quieting down.

Along with general relaxation, these techniques may result in many other benefits to both adults and children, including improved concentration, memory, and creativity. Additionally, they can help both adults and children manage stress even when they are not directly using these techniques, as they lead to a general sense of calm. Some report that such relaxation techniques improve their sleep and general well-being as well.

CHAPTER 6

Socialization

To facilitate your child's successful journey through life, teach her how to get along with all kinds of other children. Your child will need time and opportunity to practice her social and friend-making skills with children her own age. When things go awry (and they inevitably will), don't punish or scold; instead, take time to explore with what happened, what made it happen, and what she could do to get a better result next time. Parents can help with the development of social skills by coaching children with their friends, rather than intervening.

Making Friends

Social skills are among the many things children must learn, and if you've ever tried to encourage three- or four-year-olds to share, you know how challenging the process can be. Children must learn how to get along with others and to gain a sense of what others are feeling and thinking—what Daniel Siegel, MD, calls *mindsight*. The process takes time and a great deal of patience and coaching from parents.

Very young children engage in what is called parallel play. That is, they tend to sit next to each other, each playing independently. They are in the same space, and they are playing—but they are not playing together. Eventually, a child will begin to notice other children and to express curiosity about these strange beings. A little boy is likely to explore his new acquaintance by touching or poking him or by grabbing at a toy to see what he will do.

The Importance of Language and Friendship

Not surprisingly, social relationships tend to work out better when a child has learned to use his words. It also helps when a child has acquired some emotional skills and can read faces and body language to understand whether or not to approach a new person. It has been noted in several studies that girls tend to be more collaborative in their play; they talk and make rules together about how their game will go. Boys often form groups with a leader, and the chosen activity is usually physical.

School-Age Friends

When she's a little older, teach your child to ask questions to learn about new people she meets. Depending on the child's age, suggest a go-to "opener" to help break the ice. Something as simple as, "Do you like dinosaurs?" or "Want to play tag?" can help ease a child into a situation with a new friend. If she meets a boy from Pennsylvania or from Panama, look at a map or atlas with her. Show her those places and answer her questions. You want your child to develop a healthy curiosity about people and places that interest her.

Making friends also requires solid play skills. Remind your child to be willing to wait her turn, explain how her favorite toy works, and try games or activities the new friend likes, even if they are new. Talk to your pediatrician if your child seems to have problems making or keeping friends.

Learning to Share

Learning to share is important because from birth on, children are self-centered and develop a strong desire to have things. Whenever they see something new, they want it, no matter how many stuffed animals they already have. Also from about age two on, they see the world in regard to personal ownership. They talk about "my" house (where your family lives), "my" car (the car you drive), and "my" swimming pool (where you take your little girl to splash in the water). To a toddler, her bed and her room and her toys matter—a lot. She sees these items in terms of herself, and the word *mine* crops up often in her conversation.

Sharing is difficult. In fact, you may know several adults who can't do it very well. For young children (who haven't yet accepted that they are not the center of the family universe), it's often downright impossible. Sharing becomes important to parents and teachers as children reach the age of three or four and are more likely to have younger siblings or to be part of groups of children. "Share with your little brother," you might say to your daughter. Unfortunately, until she's had some training and practice, she is likely to respond by jutting out her lip and pulling harder on her toy.

Toddlers may not automatically know how to share, but they can learn quickly if you explain some basic rules, and use them systematically. Here are some sharing rules many parents explain to their children and their little visitors:

- Do not grab another child's toy unless you get permission first. Ask every time you come over, and don't assume the permission gotten once lasts for more than one visit.
- Rather than saying "no" when someone asks to play with your toys, give her hope. Say something like, "You can play with it next," or "In five minutes"

(while Mom sets the kitchen timer), or "Sure, if you let me play with your toy."

- Make sure your child understands that sharing is only temporary—she will get her toy back.
- Change the rules as the play situations change. The main thing is to teach respect for other children and treat them as you would like to be treated.

 Fact

It helps when all parents agree on the sharing rules. But even if they do not, you can always inform your child's friends that at your house there are rules for playing with each other, inside as well as outside.

You can also model sharing by showing her what it looks like:

- "Here's a cookie. I'll have a piece, and I'll share a piece with you."
- Or you can show her how to take turns: "I'll throw the ball to you, and then you throw it to me."
- You can also coach children to use words together. For example, you might say, "I can see that you want Jessie's toy. What could you say to her?" If your child says, "Please, may I have the toy?" you can smile, and then help Jessie figure out how to respond. (Please note that the answer does not

always have to be "yes." "Maybe later" is an appropriate answer, too.)

Like most of the skills and concepts adults take for granted, sharing is an art that must be practiced over and over again. As in so many other areas of life with your toddler, you can be the best teacher and example.

Teaching Delayed Gratification

Hand in hand with sharing comes the concept of delayed gratification—waiting for something (a turn with a toy, a special treat, and so on). When trying to instill in him the ability to wait for something, he will need a little help. No profound new learning can take place without a change in behavior, and that can be hard and is often resisted. Also wanting something "right now!" is as normal for a toddler as expecting to be fed every time he screams is for a newborn. But not learning patience early in life will have many negative side effects for your child later. He could become a very demanding child who may go on to demand more and more—now.

Children who have not learned to accept the word *later* sometimes have a more difficult time than others in many areas of life. In school, they may be clamoring for the teacher's attention incessantly, which can affect their progress. Later in life, they may max out their credit cards because they never learned to postpone expensive purchases until they could afford them. They may even engage in adult behaviors long before they are appropriate. But with your friendly guidance, your child can learn to increase her level of patience, delay her wishes, and wait for something until the time is right.

Short-Term Delays

Teaching a toddler to wait even a few minutes for something is a daunting task. Try to provide your toddler with the keys to success by:

1. Verbalizing his feelings for him: "You are angry because you can't have that toy now."
2. Responding to his irritation without anger: "I think I understand why."
3. Teaching him what change is needed: "Here is a solution." Then offer a replacement toy or an alternative activity.

Be sure to praise your child when he does show progress in waiting patiently for something. Your child's trust in you and your validation of his feelings will help him understand that when you say something will happen "later," it will.

Long-Term Delays

Many times, visual reminders work better than verbal ones when your child is waiting for something that is several days, weeks, or even months away. Visual reminders are like cue cards for your girl and help keep her on track, and they are also a record of the tremendous progress she is making in learning how to behave. For example, post a calendar on the refrigerator and have her mark off each day that she gets closer to that beach trip she has been begging for. When she can see the proximity of her desired goal, she can see that her waiting without making a fuss is paying off.

Playgroups

One way to help your young child socialize and practice sharing, turn-taking, and waiting is to start or join a playgroup. A playgroup is a group of children, ranging from at least two to many, that is organized for the purpose of meeting and playing under appropriate supervision. These meetings can be held in a commercial, faith-based, or private setting. Up until now, your child's inner circle may have included only parents, other close relatives, and/or the babysitter or caregiver. But now your child is ready to meet new people—her peers. For that reason, you now want to investigate all appropriate playgroups in your area.

 **Essential**

Of course, if your child already spends the time you are at work in day care, she may already have a playgroup. If you are a stay-at-home parent, however, and your child hasn't been exposed to many other children, you need to go more slowly. Introduce other children one at a time and only plan to play for short periods of time.

Many mothers of toddlers form an informal group that meets, for example, two or three times a week, on a rotating basis. While the parents watch and visit, the small children play alongside each other or—as they mature—with each other. The most beneficial playgroup arrangement is one that includes the following:

- Your child gets to spend some time in her own home environment.
- The supervision is along a one-to-one ratio.
- The parents benefit, too, as they have a chance to air their frustrations and share difficulties and triumphs.
- The cost is usually minimal. There may be a small cost for supplying the refreshments.

When you select a playgroup in a commercial or faith-based setting, you may have the assurance that the staff is well trained, but the ratio of kids to supervisors may be less than ideal—three or four toddlers to an adult, when two is a handful. Also the cost may be prohibitive, as well as the driving time. Still, check out all possibilities.

Pick 'n' Choose Playgroups

Of course, you know what will work best for you and your circumstances. But whatever choice you make, go slowly with the playgroup. Stay with your child until she is comfortable in her new setting. Depending on the degree of comfort you have with the playgroup you have selected, that may mean you will always be in the same room, or at least close by.

The best way to know if a playgroup is successful is to gauge your child's reaction. If she eagerly anticipates going to play with her new friends again, all is well. But if she is reluctant to attend the group, do not push her. Some toddlers are not ready for group play. It overwhelms them. Others can sense a lack of warmth and love for children in the supervisors. Though your toddler cannot explain the negative "vibes," you must trust their child's feelings, and either find another playgroup, hold off for a while longer, or start one yourself.

 Alert

> Never drop off your little one in a new playgroup and leave—no matter how highly recommended that group may be. Start with a trial period of a few minutes and lengthen that a few minutes at a time, with you present.

Leaving a Playgroup

Sometimes, the children in a playgroup are older than yours; they may be more rowdy, more demanding, even aggressive. Make sure the other kids are the types of children you want your child to emulate. You do not want her suddenly coming home saying bad words and hitting other children. Once you investigate what is going on, you will likely find that the other toddlers are not "bad," it's just that no one has taken the time to teach them how to behave with other children.

But unfortunately, you cannot take all the toddlers in your neighborhood under your wing. If necessary, express your concerns and reasons for leaving the playgroup to the other mothers or supervisor, and join another.

 Fact

From the age of nine months on, babies can understand the meaning of the words *no* and *yes*. After hearing "no" every time they do something that is not acceptable, they associate the word with something they should not do and "yes" with something they should do.

Curiosity

During the preschool years, even the best toddler will struggle to comply with adult expectations to behave well, make friends, and do something in a timely manner. There's just too much going on in his world. You will be far more successful at setting limits, communicating, and getting along with your toddler when you take time to be curious about who he is becoming and what his world is like. Here are some things to ponder:

- Preschoolers do not experience time in the same way adults do. Five minutes for you may feel like an hour for your toddler. If you expect patience, you will both be disappointed in the results.
- Preschoolers are far more interested in the process than the product. For example, you may want a painting to hang on your refrigerator. Your son may have found smearing the paint in his fingers satisfying

enough and may never get around to getting any on the paper.

- Preschoolers cannot tell fantasy from reality the way you can. If it happens on the movie screen or on television, it's "real" and no amount of debate can convince him otherwise. (This fact is a good reason to exercise caution where the media is concerned.)
- Preschoolers love to ask questions. While the constant stream of why and how-come can be exhausting, questions are how little children learn. Be sure to take time to listen and answer his questions.

Developmental psychologist Erik Erikson said there are two stages in children's emotional development during preschool years. At two, they learn autonomy, which is why two-year-olds love the word *no*. At three, they begin to practice initiative—the ability to make and carry out their own plans. Both of these stages create challenges for parents. Remember that it's normal development, and it is not about you.

Curiosity about your toddler's perceptions, feelings, and ideas is always a good place to begin as you solve problems and face challenges together. Take time to express curiosity before passing judgment; it will always help you parent wisely.

Easing School Anxiety

Even if your child has been able to join a playgroup and make a few toddler friends, the transition to a preschool or kindergarten setting can still be very difficult—but exciting! Visit her future school complex at a quiet time, if possible. Let her amble along the halls, count the classroom doors, maybe even peek into the cafeteria.

Later that day, ask your child what she wants to know about preschool or kindergarten. Tell her what fun lessons she will experience. Next time you swing by the school, let her lead you. Does she remember where the bathrooms and blocks are?

Long before the first bell rings, try to erase any remaining anxious thoughts she has. During the week before school starts, have her meet her new teacher—after e-mailing first to find out what time is best.

 **Essential**

Never pop into a classroom unannounced. Always communicate with the teacher before you come to visit. Even though your girl's school may loudly proclaim its open-door policy, no teacher wants to be interrupted during work.

While getting your child acclimated to her school before the opening day, check on her listening and sharing skills. Most important, tell her that her teacher is similar to her parent. At home the motto is "do what Mom or Dad tells you." At school, it is "do what the teacher tells you."

CHAPTER 7

Fostering a Child's Growing Independence

Learning to trust others is a major developmental task that has ramifications carrying over into adult years. You may have friends or have known people who cannot trust, no matter what, and sadly, they often have miserable lives. You have the ability to create an emotional environment for your child that will enable him to be a happy, independent adult. It's an important job!

Learning to Trust

Being able to trust caregivers enough to accept their comfort, help, rules, and guidance is critical for toddlers' overall emotional well-being. This foundation of trust should have been established during infancy through the unwavering love and nurturing devotion of parents and other caregivers. Toddlers' growing trust in themselves complicates their trust in parents, which wanes as toddlers put more trust in their own feelings, thoughts, and ideas. Emotional swings intensify as youngsters try to balance their trust in themselves and in their parents. In order to maintain a strong relationship when trust wanes during the toddler years:

- Be consistent and true to your word.
- Invite toddlers to participate in decisions that affect them by giving them some choices.
- Soothe upsets by cuddling, kissing, and speaking kindly.
- Communicate your understanding that some rules and limits are upsetting.
- Let your child's upset be her own. In other words, be aware of what is your child's emotion and what is your emotion.
- Let your child know you love her even if you dislike some of the things she does (criticize the behavior, not the child).

- Show with your actions that your love and respect for her continue even when you are angry with her.
- Apologize if you become harsh and critical—this will help your child learn it is okay to make mistakes and to apologize for them.

 Alert

Developmental psychologists agree that a nurturing parent-child relationship is critical for toddlers. This single relationship influences youngsters' relationships with other authority figures from today's teachers to tomorrow's bosses. It also impacts how they get along with siblings, peers, friends, and future mates.

Parents as Safe Havens

Psychologist Harry Harlow conducted groundbreaking research that demonstrated how critical a nurturing parent is for children's emotional development. His studies on young monkeys have important implications for child rearing. Harlow separated newborn monkeys from their parents and raised them in cages that were barren except for a wire mesh structure. When the little orphans nursed from a baby bottle, they would cling to the wire mesh as if it were a mother.

Despite adequate nutrition, it soon became evident that the emotional development of the little ones was seriously distorted. When Harlow placed something frightening in a cage, such as a noisy wind-up toy, each orphan would flee to a corner, hide its face, and tremble in terror, unable to summon the courage to approach the object for a closer look. Later, when other baby monkeys were placed in the cage of a little orphan, it didn't know how to play or interact with them. When the deprived orphans grew up, their emotional development was so stunted they couldn't even figure out how to mate.

Young monkeys raised with their mother were much more able to cope with the wind-up toy trauma. They fled to their mother for comfort when the frightening toy first appeared but soon became brave enough to approach it. Each time they lost courage, they ran back to their mother for support and to regroup. Within moments they were happily playing with the new toy.

The parent-child dynamics of these monkeys, Harlow realized, mirrors what happens in the human world. A caregiver to whom the toddler is attached serves as the child's island of safety when a stranger comes into the house or when he feels frightened for any reason. Once a frightened child has spent a few moments with his human security blanket, he ventures forth with renewed courage.

Stranger Anxiety

Hand in hand with separation anxiety comes stranger anxiety. Shy, fearful behavior around strangers (meaning anyone other than the immediate family and trusted caregivers) starts around eight to twelve months of age. It peaks by about eighteen months and gradually lessens and disappears by age three except in the shyest youngsters. Negative reactions during this period tend to be more pronounced toward men than women, and least pronounced toward other children.

When a child is distressed about a "stranger" (who can actually be a relative or neighbor the child has met many times before), hold her on your lap to help her feel safe and don't pressure her to interact. Once out of the limelight and given time to observe the new people, most toddlers grow bolder about approaching household guests. Tell Aunt Emily and Uncle Bob not to take the rejection personally.

 **Question**

How can I help my child interact with strangers?
Support your child's desire not to be touched by not pressuring your child to socialize with visitors. Let her get used to new people, or even family members she has been around before, to see if she warms up to them. You might even teach relatives or new friends to try to distract your child by sitting next to you and playing with a favorite toy while avoiding eye contact. That technique might help get your child slowly accustomed to the new person.

If your guests venture to hug or kiss your child, intervene if it's clear your child is uncomfortable. This is not the time to teach toddlers about "dangerous" strangers, or "good" versus "bad" touching, however. They're too young to understand these concepts, and emphasizing the issue may make them more afraid of people than they already are. Suggest the person blow a kiss instead—that way, your child sees that Aunt Emily cares about her but stays at a distance that makes your child feel safe.

The Importance of Healthy Contact

Though your child may be uncomfortable with an unfamiliar person's touch, he likely craves yours, even as he becomes more independent. In fact, Harlow's studies on young monkeys yielded another important finding: Little orphans deprived of the warmth of a live mother monkey were less healthy than their peers. Researchers have found that this, too, has parallels in the world of humans. Youngsters in orphanages often have poor weight gain. Some sicken if they are not held and cuddled regularly, even if they are otherwise cared for. This medical condition is called "failure to thrive."

Experts now agree that loving human touch, "contact comfort," is a basic need, as important as food and water for physical and emotional development. Contact comfort has important health benefits for people of all ages. By learning to reach out for a hug, toddlers learn a skill that will help them stay healthy!

Soothing Touches

When young toddlers are upset, words alone aren't enough to comfort them because of their limited comprehension of speech. They need:

- A shoulder to cry on when they are sad.
- A lap to bury their face in when they are afraid.

- Arms to hug them and provide comfort and reassurance.
- Back rubs to soothe them when they are ill.
- Tickles to cheer them up.

Hugging, kissing, rocking, rubbing, and cuddling have relaxing and soothing physical effects. A toddler's pulse rate slows and respiration becomes more even. Endorphins released into the bloodstream provide a sense of well-being. Studies show that youngsters in intensive care recover more rapidly if they are regularly massaged, stroked, held, or otherwise able to reap the benefits of human touch.

Soothing touches are also important for building trust and strengthening the child's emotional attachment to the primary caregiver. These touches will also help your toddler feel brave enough to approach new situations independently when he is ready.

Separation Anxiety

Separation anxiety is different from stranger anxiety and usually strikes at around twelve to twenty-four months. Your baby suddenly seems miserable whenever you are out of sight, even if you have just briefly gone to the next room.

At first, the best way of dealing with separation anxiety is to simply go along with it. If your baby is clingy, pick her up and cuddle her. If she wants to explore, smile and nod at her explorations from across the room. If she doesn't want to leave you, pick her up and move her from room to room as you go. You can start to practice short separations, though, leaving the room for a few seconds, calling out to her, and quickly returning.

As she gets bigger, you can try other reassuring methods to alleviate separation anxiety:

- Keep up a constant conversation if you step out of the room because she may not be so worried if she can hear your voice.
- Play hide-and-seek (peek out from your hiding place and call her) to get her used to you appearing and disappearing.
- Use a "lovey"—a special blanket or toy—to help you and your baby through this phase. The lovey will remind your baby of you when you're not around. (More on this topic next.)
- Don't delay or draw out your departures. Tell your child you love her, give her a hug and a kiss, and be on your way. The quicker you leave, the faster the child's caregiver can begin offering fun activities and distractions to help her move on.

Separation anxiety will come and go for years, so get used to it. It doesn't mean that you should never leave your baby or that she's miserable the whole time you are gone. Find a babysitter you trust, someone who is willing to actively work to calm your baby down when you leave, and know that the tears don't leave a permanent scar on her psyche. Usually, if it's a familiar babysitter, your child will calm down and enjoy herself after a few minutes.

Comfort Objects

Did you have a special teddy or blankie when you were small? If you can remember that far back, you can empathize with how important those special objects are to your toddler. Having them nearby can make transitions from home to car to day care to the store and back home manageable. Without them, it's a disaster. It's common for toddlers to become so attached to a particular object that they can't bear to be separated from it. The object doesn't have to be something soft, like a blanket. Some youngsters develop affection for a toy truck or flashlight. What matters is the bond the child has formed with it. These special objects help toddlers cope with situations that require a separation from their parent, such as going to day care or to bed.

Parents may be frustrated if their toddler insists on having the same toy at his side every moment of the day and sleeps with it at night. As the months go by and their child's grip on Mr. Teddy or his "blankie" remains as tight as ever, they begin to picture their toddler walking up to the podium at high school graduation clutching the bedraggled toy under his arm. Fortunately, no such incident has ever been recorded, and there's no reason to believe your child will be the first!

The social pressures of kindergarten can be counted on to bring a quick end to the love affair with an inanimate object—at least in public. Lots of teens still cuddle their teddy at night, so don't worry about your child's need for a comfort object, and don't push your child to relinquish it. If your child seems overly attached to a comfort object, try to give more hugs and spend more time cuddling.

 **Essential**

> A comfort or transitional object is the popular term for a blanket, piece of clothing, toy, or other object that serves as a child's "surrogate mother." If your child derives comfort from one, respect this important relationship! It has deep, emotional meaning to the child, just as your favorite items have deep, particular meaning for you. Although almost any object will do, a blanket, having several duplicates ready for when they wear out, makes a great comfort object.

"Me Do It"

Coping with the toddler's drive for independence can be hard for parents, and it's even harder for toddlers. Mother Nature can be capricious. She pushes youngsters to be independent even when they lack the skills needed to do things by themselves. The same child who is determined to put a puzzle together by himself may lack the fine motor coordination needed to do it. One minute he is raging at the parent who dares to try to help; the next minute he recognizes his inadequacy and rages at the parent for *not* helping. Then, when the parent once again tries to show the toddler how to do it, Mother Nature whispers in the toddler's ear that he must do it himself, and he is again raging at the parent for having touched his puzzle. Now that the parent has defiled it, the youngster wants nothing to do with it.

 Fact

Allow more time for getting ready in the morning and before going out in case your toddler suddenly decides she must handle some of the preparations herself, but don't allow your child to become a little dictator. Seize control when your child's attempts to be independent are inappropriate.

Children in the throes of an independence struggle put their parents in no-win situations because toddlers are caught in a series of no-win situations themselves. Their emotions vacillate wildly and their behavior becomes erratic as they insist on being independent one minute and regress to helpless dependency the next.

Toddlers in this stage may revert to the familiar comforts of thumb sucking and demand their long-discarded baby bottles back, but then treat your attempts to help them cut their meat as a major affront to their dignity. Long-resolved issues such as the need to wear a seat belt and hold Mommy's hand while crossing the street may become battlegrounds once again.

Although toddlers must be allowed to try to do more for themselves, having too much power frightens them. They are not ready to be independent, and they know it.

The Problem with Too Much Praise

While it's important to praise your child for his successes, resist the impulse to constantly praise simple, ordinary acts. It has the effect of making your toddler unnecessarily dependent on your opinion, when becoming a full, separate person involves making up one's own mind and doing things, simply because it's the thing to do. Too much praise can actually create an individual who is insecure in the world.

 **Essential**

> There's nothing wrong with saying "Good" to teach a child to do things in a certain way. Certainly there are "right" and "wrong" ways to do many things. However, giving positive feedback in situations that are meant to be pure fun can cause toddlers to turn play sessions into grim tests of their competence.

Children with good self-esteem feel pleased with themselves. When evaluating their own behavior, they feel they measure up to their personal expectations. But praise can actually serve to undermine self-esteem. First-born children, whose parents are apt to applaud each small gurgle and goo and record each new accomplishment in their bulging baby book, tend to be the least emotionally secure and suffer more problems with self-esteem than the rest of the brood, whose successes receive far less attention. Meanwhile, the middle child, typically lost in a no-man's land between the accomplished older sibling and the darling baby, has a harder time finding ways to impress. Yet youngsters sandwiched in the middle of the pack tend to be more self-confident.

The following parent comments point out some of the pitfalls of praise:

- "I like the bright colors in your drawing" suggests to the child that to please the parent, he should use bright colors. Expressing interest and asking a neutral question such as "Tell me about your picture" enables the child to share his drawing and his feelings about it without having his choice of crayons judged.
- If the parent exclaims, "Good catch!" when the ball lands in the toddler's arms, it's understandable why he becomes upset when it lands on the floor on subsequent tries; the youngster assumes they are "bad" catches.
- "Good girl!" the parent says when the toddler uses the potty by herself. This kind of evaluation— "You're good because you did what I wanted"—can cause toddlers who are in the throes of a struggle over independence to respond by refusing to use the potty thereafter. Instead, try, "You should be proud of yourself." Although that still conveys your opinion, it encourages the child to evaluate herself in a positive light rather than to focus exclusively on your opinion.

CHAPTER 8

Fixes for Naughty Behaviors

Understanding what causes bad behaviors is half the battle in dealing with it. You must understand your child's behavior before you can try to change it. These emotional outbursts can be difficult to deal with and usually occur when you are least able to deal patiently with them. In this chapter, you will learn about what you can expect from a variety of common behavior challenges.

Hitting and Biting

Boys are usually more prone to physical aggression and competition than are girls—but every parent needs to nip this behavior in the bud. Children may kick, bite, or throw things when they feel frustrated or tired. Speech experts believe that some aggressive activity may be related to the development of language; children who are slower to speak clearly often experience frustration and express it in the form of anger or defiance.

Your child needs to learn that hurting himself, another person, or property is never acceptable. But hurting *him* will not teach that lesson. Instead, always take a moment to calm down first, and then help him do the same. (You will learn more about positive time-out later in this chapter.) Remove your child gently from the situation or from other children if necessary. Then, when both you and he are able to talk calmly, look together for solutions to the problem.

If other children are involved, it is helpful to explore what they might have been feeling. You can also tell your child how you are feeling: "I feel sad and worried when you kick the dog." Or, "It hurts when you hit me, and I cannot allow you to do that." Stay calm; raising your own voice never helps.

Whining

Another behavior that can become a problem at home, in school, and in life is a tendency to whine. When a car whines, it needs something—a checkup, lubricant, or an overhaul. When a toddler whines, she needs an adjustment, too. Maybe she has learned that her plaintive utterances get big results, but in the long run, whiners are annoying and people avoid them. Resist the urge to give in to her whining so she learns that the behavior will not get her anything. Praise her when she asks for something in a polite, non-whiny fashion.

Potty Mouth

Children only use words they have heard someone else say. If the naughty words have come from outside the household, the best strategy is simply to ignore them, which ups the odds that they'll go away. Otherwise, you'll spark your toddler's curiosity about the magic of a word that has the ability to make you laugh or get angry, increasing the likelihood he'll use it more often.

 Alert

> Even if naughty words don't bother you, they can upset teachers, other parents, and children enough to dampen your youngster's social life. Insist on a healthy vocabulary.

If the offensive words don't disappear on their own, or if he's using words he's heard at home, eliminate these no-nos from the family vocabulary before they become a habit. Tell your child that saying that word is a no-no and provide a brief time-out. To help yourself and other family members clean up their vocabularies, say, "Oops, somebody just said a no-no," and put your child in charge of walking the offender to his bedroom for a brief time-out.

Profanity can be a particular challenge for parents of older boys. Cursing and rough language, like other risky behavior, may be viewed by boys as a trait of masculinity. Boys feel manly and sophisticated when they let loose with a barrage of four-letter words. You might tell your son that you would prefer not to hear that language—and you don't want him speaking that way to teachers or other adults. This lesson will be much easier to teach, of course, if you refrain from using profanity yourself. Then, help your child list a few good substitute words, such as *darn, shoot,* and *rats* for the four-letter words that are so commonplace these days.

Interrupting and/or Not Listening

Most parents are delighted and proud when their little boy politely says "please," "thank you," and "excuse me." Parents are a bit less delighted when the preschool years pass and children seem to shed their manners along with their diapers. Suddenly, the child ignores you, or interrupts conversations left and right. If you believe that manners and common courtesy are important, be sure you continue to model and teach them in your family. Your child is far more likely to practice good manners if you show her how.

For example, if your daughter interrupts you while you are having a conversation with another adult or are talking on the phone, designate a signal. Holding up one hand means you need five more minutes. Teach her to set the kitchen timer for that period. Then she can wait patiently until the bell goes off.

Patience in the Digital Age

You will need a lot of patience as your toddler masters various tasks. You will need to take a deep breath from time to time and realize that it takes a lot of time and repetition for your little one to master pulling on socks, eating with utensils, and waiting in line at the bank or post office.

Likewise, your child needs to learn patience. In *Generation Text: Raising Well-Adjusted Kids in an Age of Instant Everything*, psychologist Michael Osit warns that in an immediate-gratification world, your child has to learn the difference between wants and needs. Your toddler may insist, "I need your iPad now" with the same insistence that he wants something to eat when he's hungry. As the parent, you help him learn the difference. Everyone has to learn that delay is a part of life and nobody always gets what he wants.

Accepting the disappointments of life, like not being able to play with the iPad one more time, is a part of gradual maturity. Osit describes it as learning to exercise a muscle. Little by little, parent and child get through the anguish of realizing that life does not always provide what is wanted. Clear, firm guidance during the toddler years prevents later nightmares.

You Set the Example

You, as the parent, need to exercise the patience muscle as much as the child, as it's certainly no fun attracting the stares of other library patrons while your child is in the throes of a screaming tantrum. During such difficult times, remember that you're both learning and exercising the patience muscle. The child needs for you to be the wise, experienced adult and to help contain the rage and frustration of being unable to wait.

How do you teach a toddler to hold it together and wait? Be calm, not angry. Parental anger triggers more emotional upset in tots, making difficult situations all the more taxing for them. Remember that there is nothing wrong with a child wanting something. When guilt and shame are added to toddlers' frustration over not having their desires fulfilled, their stress increases and that makes it more difficult for them to wait.

Give Reasons

Explain why your toddler must wait. It is all too easy for toddlers to conclude that their parents are withholding things and privileges capriciously. That compounds their frustration.

Furthermore, reasonable explanations enable toddlers to apply what they learn in one situation to another. Tots in church may not understand when a parent says, "You must be quiet now. People are talking to God with their hearts and you're disturbing them. You can talk later." But as their language skills improve and they continue to hear explanations, they will eventually understand. Then they can use their knowledge to figure out how to act in other situations where people are concentrating, such as at a live performance, instead of needing an adult to tell them what to do at every moment.

Sometimes parents can't give explanations because they aren't clear about the reasons for certain rules themselves. They only know they must be observed. If you can't supply a reason at the moment, think about it later. When you come up with a reason, share it with your toddler: "Remember yesterday when I said you couldn't use the computer until later? That's because too much computer use isn't good for kids. Kids need to play to exercise their bodies and minds." There is sometimes a benefit to sharing reasons later rather than during a contentious moment. Children are more able to listen and consider the parents' words more objectively.

If children are admonished when they have difficulty waiting but hear nothing when they do wait patiently, they won't have the motivation to try again. When your toddler finally calms down after a scene over wanting something now, remember to point out his accomplishment. An hour after calm is restored, say, "I'm proud you were able to stop crying when I told you that you couldn't paint until after lunch. I'll make sure you get to do it after we eat."

Let Me Be Naked!

Lots of toddlers decide clothes are something they'd rather do without. Every time parents turn around, they find their little one has managed to wriggle out of her clothes again. The dislike of clothing isn't surprising. If children are warm enough, they will feel much more comfortable with the freedom of movement that comes from being in bare skin. It may not be a problem if toddlers want to run around the house in their birthday suit, though this can get pretty messy if they're not toilet-trained. (That's an incentive some parents have successfully used with determined strippers: If you use the toilet, birthday suits are allowed at home.)

At Home and Away

Regardless of what policies are in force at home, parents should insist that toddlers observe the social niceties of keeping their clothes on outside the house. Even if you don't care, other parents will be offended. Dressing toddlers in blouses that button up the back, pants with belts, and double-knotting shoelaces can slow down little strippers so parents can catch them before they completely disrobe.

 Essential

If your child acts up when you're out and about, it's important to offer the same response you would if you were at home. Don't give into demands simply because you're embarrassed about the public outburst.

However, there's no need to be upset or to shame them about it. Since they're too young to comprehend adult views on the subject, instilling guilt might make them feel that their body is bad or dirty. It should be enough to firmly state, "Undressing outside the house is a no-no!" and to put their clothes back on again and again until they get the message. Don't comfort them if they howl; there are times when staying dressed is nonnegotiable. Also, avoid attempting to make dressing fun. Otherwise, they may conclude that removing their clothes is a way to initiate a great game.

Time-Outs

Providing time-outs is an excellent teaching device to help toddlers learn to adhere to important rules and regain control when they are unable to contain themselves. Tell your toddler to sit down until she can settle down, or ignore her, and observe the limit you have set (usually a minute per year of age).

 Fact

Many parents send toddlers to their room for time-out, but keep in mind that any designated area will do as a time-out area. The point of time-out is to teach, not to punish, although until children learn the advantages of being contained, they may feel punished. You'll have to judge the situation for yourself, keeping in mind your child's temperament. Remember that time-out is supposed to be time-out from attention and is also a chance for your child to cool down.

The rule of thumb is to assign one minute of time-out per year of age, so a two-year-old should be required to sit for two minutes at most. Some mature toddlers will be able to sit longer. If toddlers weren't upset to begin with, they may become very angry about being prevented from engaging in the activity they have chosen. You may wish to start the clock only after the child has settled down, but be careful that one time-out doesn't turn into an all-day affair.

When the child has regained control, discuss the event that precipitated the time-out to help her learn from the experience so she knows what to do if the same situation arises in the future. It helps to begin the discussion by praising the toddler for having regained control. Besides starting the discussion on a positive note, praise helps little ones focus on their important accomplishments, and keeps both the parent and child from being overly focused on the misdeeds.

Reviewing what transpired and figuring out what to do differently is beyond younger toddlers and will be too hard for older toddlers until they are familiar with the process. In the beginning, you may have to do most or all of the talking for your toddler:

Do you know why I sent you to time-out? Blank stare

Because you turned on the TV after I told you not to. Blank stare

You can't watch any more TV today. Too much TV watching isn't good for kids, remember? Blank stare

The TV needs to stay off, okay? Nods

There's still no guarantee that the toddler understood the question. If she turns on the TV again, the parent will need to assign another minute or two in time-out. The point of time-out is to teach several important lessons children can use throughout their lives:

1. Important rules must be followed.
2. If people disregard rules, there are consequences, which may be unpleasant.
3. If people don't control themselves, someone else will control them.
4. When people are upset and out of control, taking a brief time-out can help them calm down.

Most children learn the value of time-outs in short order. In fact, once they have become accustomed to the procedure, some toddlers will begin sitting down or running off to their room when they are upset over a parental demand or prohibition. During their self-imposed time-out, they will finish crying and re-emerge, settled, a few minutes later.

Spanking

While spankings may more quickly control a child who is repeatedly engaging in forbidden behavior, the fatal flaw is that the parent is controlling the child's behavior. Children need to learn to control their own behavior. Also, parents who spank often do it when they are mad, and have lost control themselves.

❗ Alert

You will have to make up your own mind about the place of spanking in disciplining your toddler, and seek consensus with your spouse, relatives, and caretakers. Some parents believe that the only way to create a non-violent world is to engage in no violence in the home. Sometimes your disapproval and consistent caring is enough to shape your child's behavior.

Although some people think that spanking is a reasonable course of action in situations involving imminent danger, such as running into the street, reaching for a hot stove, provoking an animal, or running around a swimming pool, a firm "no" is a reasonable alternative. Since it is thought that spanking can make kids more aggressive later in life and because spanking has never been a proven or reliable punishment technique, the American Academy of Pediatrics is firmly against spanking children for any reason.

CHAPTER 9

Girl-Specific Issues

Core gender identity is formed during the toddler years. Children may go through phases, but by age two they should have a conception of themselves as being female. Toddler girls typically identify people's sex by their peripheral characteristics, such as clothing, hairstyle, or use of makeup; they don't have a real conception of what it means to be female. Most modern parents want to avoid raising their children in accordance with old gender stereotypes. They want their daughters to have a positive self-image, be comfortable asserting themselves, and have wider career aspirations.

Girls and Emotions

Research by the California neuropsychiatrist Luann Brizendine—as reported in *Newsweek* (July 31, 2006)—may explain how brain chemistry and genetic wiring can especially influence women's actions and feelings. Dr. Brizendine's work focuses on why girls act like girls, which by no means implies inferiority. Among the various brain parts this scientist has her eyes on is the hypothalamus, a region of the brain the size of a cherry that is responsible for hormonal control. In females it springs into action earlier than in males, causing girls to enter puberty sooner than boys, and making girls more sensitive to the fluctuations of their hormones. While this study is ongoing, it may shed light on why your girl experiences emotional turbulence and mood swings.

Dealing with Developing Personalities

Even if your child's personality is not the one you wished for, if you could, it is still *her* personality, so rejoice. What personality is exactly has been much debated. However, most experts agree that it consists of a person's traits, habits, and experiences.

Although a child's personality arises out of the interplay of her heredity and environment, it encompasses the following aspects:

- Intelligence
- Temperament

- Motivation
- Emotion

Intelligence and its various areas of manifestation in school children are wide-ranging and can be difficult to define broadly. As for temperament, consider your child's nature and responses to common situations. For example, some children are easily upset over what appears to be minor, while others shrug off most annoyances, even major ones.

In regard to motivation and emotion, think about your child's hopes, likes and dislikes, and feelings. Her likes and feelings come into play the older she gets and the more her individual preferences emerge. These preferences may influence how she acts. Here are some common female personality types and information on what makes each one tick.

The Tomboy or Tough Girl

If your daughter has tomboy tendencies, she makes herself seen and heard from early on, not by breaking into uncontrollable sobs, but by being feisty. In most people's opinions, she acts more like a boy than a girl. From the moment she gets up in the morning, there is commotion since she rarely tiptoes. Usually she jumps over a chair on her way into a room. She prefers to play with a ball or a toy truck than with dolls. If you insist on giving her a doll, she rigs up a catapult out of twigs and rubber bands, and sends her shooting through the yard.

If your daughter has tomboy tendencies, accept her with open arms and make sure her teachers do, too. Tell her she makes you happy just the way she is. But watch out: If she has older brothers, she may engage in rough-and-tumble play with them. Not being as big and strong as they are, she may get hurt more quickly. Or she may best them in various kinds of physical contests, so be prepared for her brothers' long faces.

 Fact

> No matter how tomboyish your daughter acts, instill in her the appropriateness of dress when appropriate. Depending on the occasion, she should always wear a suitable outfit. That does not necessarily mean a skirt and blouse or dress—it can be a dressy pants ensemble or whatever else the occasion calls for.

As far as your tomboy's appearance, she may get just as dirty as boys, or more so, and revel in the process. Often a tomboy prefers blue jeans and T-shirts to skirts and dresses, which can be a benefit. Buy her the clothes she wants. They are usually easier to take care of than girly outfits, may be less costly, and last longer.

HOW TO FOSTER HER GROWTH

Many parents agree on a compromise when it comes to the clothing of a tomboy. They have an every-other-day rule. That means on some days they choose their daughter's attire. On others, she is free to wear her favorite sweatshirt and ripped jeans. For her birthday or holiday gifts, ask what she wants. Whether it is overalls or a toolbox filled with the latest tools, fulfill her heart's desire.

Many tomboys go through developmental stages that may include:

- A slow but increasing liking for activities, clothing, and behaviors usually associated with boys.
- A peak period when she may wear her hair in a boyish style, prefer to play only with boys, and insist on being called by a unisex form of her name, such as Alex for Alexandra or Sam for Samantha, or she may switch to a male-only name such as Derek.
- A switchback to more middle-of-the road behaviors such as acting like a traditional girl sometimes and like a boy at other times.

Not all tomboys go through stages. Some tough girls stay the way they developed from early on and grow into confident, independent-thinking, success-oriented young women. As adults, former tomboys are often much in demand because they are usually strong-willed, are high achievers, and can do so many useful things from changing the oil in a car to installing a new sink, thereby saving money and time. Most of all, they are empowered in all situations. Wow—what a great asset.

The Ballerina or Skater

One of the best things you can do for your daughter is to encourage her to grow into what she is meant to be. You will never know what your daughter could become unless you validate her early wishes and encourage her as she tries to follow the path of her innermost passions. In the case of a girl who is drawn to being a ballerina or skater, she may relish the grace and beauty that dancers and skaters exemplify. You simply supply what she needs and watch her advance.

 **Essential**

Be alert to the fact that tomboys can get teased not only by girls but also by boys. Teach her a few handy comebacks, such as, in regard to her outfits, "It's the latest style," or in regard to her rough play, "I'm practicing for the Olympics," or in general, "Don't you wish you could be like me?"

HOW TO FOSTER HER GROWTH

There are so many ways you can foster your girl's interest in dance steps or skates, whether they're meant for an ice rink or a skate park. Classes abound in ballet, jazz, rhythm, tap, modern dance, and all forms of skating. The great thing about getting your girl involved in these activities is that they increase her flexibility, poise, and gracefulness. Her body, and her self-confidence, benefit as well. Another plus: these activities are available in many locations in your community. Thus, if your daughter enjoys them, check out the many dance schools and sports complexes around. Then sign her up for a trial class.

Costumes for dancing and skating can cost huge amounts, over and above the fees required for the lessons.

No matter how determined your girl is to be a great dancer or skater, start slowly. Often after-school programs offer introductory classes. In middle school, dance may be offered as a subject, and she can try her skating flair at a public ice rink before getting too deeply involved. Always leave the door open for your daughter to develop an interest in something entirely new. So much has to do with the development of her body and spirit. Growth in a girl's talents is rarely straightforward. It may involve several side paths to other interests. But that is what makes parenting so fascinating. It broadens you just as your daughter broadens her interests. She may decide that dancing and skating are not for her. Instead, she may want to take up tae kwon do or some other sport. That's why it is good to try a lot of different activities when your kids are young and to try and not specialize too early.

 Fact

Do not insist that your daughter continue to take dance or skating lessons if she loses interest. Children change their minds about what they like many times, so it is best not to pay for a program far in advance if possible. Go with a week-to-week payment plan and have another activity in mind that you can introduce next.

The Athlete or Outdoor Girl

If your girl has some or a lot of athletic ability, you are again fortunate because there are so many opportunities for her. Whether it is tae kwon do, soccer, or lacrosse, be glad your girl has found something she is passionate about.

She may enjoy the physical aspects of the sport, or being outside, or being in a team environment with some close friends. As she grows, she may even travel to games, meets, or matches outside her town, which can be a fun and enriching experience.

HOW TO FOSTER HER GROWTH

The best way to motivate your athletic girl is by taking her to places where kids play sports. Besides the usual sports venues in many schools and towns, most communities have YMCAs that offer a large menu of activities that fall under leisure (for fun) or enrichment (more advanced skills) categories. Most often girls are divided into groups based on age, grade level, and interests and abilities. For very little money, they can find out if they have an interest in basketball, volleyball, softball, field hockey, and other team sports.

Individual sports such as diving may also be offered, in addition to swimming. Your daughter can have a whole array of athletic pursuits to explore before she decides on cross-country running or downhill skiing, if she likes being outdoors.

As long as she enjoys her choice of sports and is not overcommitted, you can relax—not that there will be much free time for you to do so. Parents of budding female athletes frequently have to make sacrifices. When the tryouts for the various teams are over and your girl has been chosen, her schedule may change, as may yours.

The Artist or Crafts Enthusiast

Not every girl likes chasing after a ball or cycling her heart out. Some enjoy various forms of arts or crafts. They may be content to sit in the den and doodle, sketch, or write. Or they fashion objects out of Play-Doh, or stitch together a new outfit for their stuffed toys. Girls with this wonderful ability to entertain themselves are easy to satisfy. Paper and crayons are easy to come by. Modeling clay and cloth remnants cost almost nothing. All you need to do is give your young artist or crafts enthusiast a corner in your house as a hobby station, and she is in business. Try to keep her active, though, even if it isn't in a formal sport.

HOW TO FOSTER HER GROWTH

Art as a subject is taught in most schools, often from the middle grades on up. Some schools also hold monthly art exhibits. Others schedule performances where your artistic daughter can read her poetry or show off her blossoming acting talent or the props she painted for the drama club. If your girl's school is underfunded in the art department, check out the art center in your community. Research the best after-school programs for your creative daughter. The wonderful thing about having a daughter who is talented in arts and crafts is that she is never bored.

Your arts and crafts–oriented girl can always find something enjoyable and useful to do. Just giving her a box of buttons, pieces of colored ribbons, construction paper, and glue can get her started. Before long she will be able to:

- Design and print greeting cards for the whole family.
- Update old T-shirts with velvet cutouts and sparkles.
- Dash off a short story and illustrate it for the kinder-garten class in her school.

To know that you are raising such a productive and self-sufficient girl who has a wealth of creative talent is a special joy.

 **Essential**

If your girl complains about being teased for being a science geek, tell her to take it as a compliment. Down the road she will be the one cashing in, while the teasers may come crawling, asking her for a job.

The Science, Math, and Computer Geek

Congratulations to you if your daughter is into science, math, engineering, or computers. For one thing, she can probably teach you a thing or two. And best of all, since there are still so few girls deeply committed to those fields, her likelihood of getting scholarships and grants later will skyrocket. Do what you can to keep your daughter's early interest from flagging. Try to supply her with the latest tech equipment. But again, make sure she gets some physical activity each day.

HOW TO FOSTER HER GROWTH

Depending on her age, you might be able to enroll your child in a community or school-sponsored class to further her interest. If she loves her digital camera, see if a local camera store offers a Saturday course (that would be appropriate for children) on taking great pictures. If she wants to try some basic science experiments, ask her teacher to recommend some age-appropriate options, then do your best to facilitate them at home.

If you don't share your child's interest in science or computers, look around at your immediate family or circle of friends. Perhaps an uncle, aunt, or cousin has knowledge they can share with your daughter. Or it could be a good way to broaden your own horizons and learn something new.

Girls and Moms

The mother-daughter relationship can be one of the most amazing and magical relationships in the world. If it works well, it is exponentially better than any other relationship because it interconnects two people who have a similar talent—the ability to share their emotions and feelings—and yet are a generation apart. Therefore, one of them has the wisdom of experience and years, and the other has the freshness of youth. With a healthy bond, a mother and her daughter may find that they have the skills and smarts to overcome any problem or challenge they face.

Clashes and Challenges

The special relationship between a mother and daughter is primal, the first one the daughter experiences. As she matures, the daughter starts focusing more on her friends and later perhaps on men, but her original love connection is always with her mother. After all, she receives so much from her mom—food, shelter, and nurturing, to name just a few things. From babyhood on, a girl also consciously or subconsciously patterns herself after her mother in speech, mannerisms, and other means of expression. Of course, that can cause clashes and challenges.

 Fact

In recent years the term *matrophobia* has cropped up frequently in literature. It denotes the quite common fear of a young woman of growing up to be just like her mother.

One of the most common problems between mothers and daughters is the fight over control. The daughter feels that the mother is always trying to control her, and the mother has trouble accepting her little girl as an independent person. In addition, many mothers are not sure of who *they* are, so they focus all their energies on the person their daughter is turning out to be. A mother who is secure and comfortable as a person will be a better role model for a daughter than a mother who is constantly badgering a daughter to improve herself.

Two headstrong women who are only one generation apart can come to many disagreements and end up in a battle based on control and rebellion. Remember: What worked for you does not always work for your daughter, but you must set a pattern early on of quickly settling any disagreements with your daughter. This pattern should include compromising, laying out the pros and cons of a decision she has to make, and admitting it when you are wrong.

 **Essential**

Receiving a text from their parents is preferable to receiving a phone call from them by many teenagers because—without a voice being involved and due to the shorter length—it tends to be less intense, less emotional, and less demanding.

Resolve Clashes

The more often a healthy process of conflict resolution between you and your daughter occurs, the smoother the relationship. But even then difficulties can arise. One major stumbling block is the silent treatment. Ditch it at all costs. Silence does nothing but erect a wall, or an abyss, between you and your girl. Keep communicating even if your daughter turns mum. If you are afraid of opening your mouth for fear of saying something to her you will regret later, turn to a note pad, your computer, or simply text message.

In fact, by writing down what is on your mind, you have a chance to examine the words before you show or send them to your daughter. When you speak, the thought process is often minimal because words can fly out of your mouth. But the simple act of committing your thoughts to a sheet of paper, a computer screen, or a cell phone screen slows down the flow of verbiage. So the message sent will be reduced in harshness.

Keep Communication Open

It is *your* job to initiate the flow of communication after your daughter has cut it off. If you do not make the effort, both of you will feel helpless and hopeless. Give your daughter power by showing her that you are not afraid to tackle a touchy subject or whatever stands between you. It is always a sign of strength to broach a difficult topic. But verbalizing hurt feelings can be tricky for both mother and daughter.

Remember when communicating with your daughter that not only the words you choose carry weight, but also your tone of voice and facial demeanor. You never want to come across as overly critical. The written word, thought out beforehand, is much more neutral.

Skills for Connecting with Your Daughter

A daughter's bond with her mother is one of the deepest, most enduring relationships she will experience in her lifetime. It should also be one of the healthiest and most supportive.

Here are some suggestions for building a strong, loving connection with your girl:

- **Listen and observe.** Good mothers are willing to spend time just listening and watching. Ask "what" and "how" questions to draw your daughter out. Let her finish her thoughts before offering suggestions or advice.
- **Spend time just being together. Relationships require time.** You must be willing to hang out, play, and do things face-to-face with your daughter. Have at least fifteen minutes a day that belong just to your daughter.
- **Respond to your daughter's cues.** When she says, "I can do it myself, Mom!" teach the necessary skills, be sure she's safe, and allow her to try. Skills and experience build self-esteem.
- **Be curious about her interests.** If your daughter loves an activity, sharing her enthusiasm is a wonderful way to build connection. Watch her favorite sport with her; admire the painting she made. Understanding your daughter's world will keep you connected.
- **Know her friends.** There is no better way to learn about your daughter than to watch her at play with her friends. As your daughter grows, welcome her friends into your home. If she can bring her life to you, she is less likely to feel the need to hide it from you.
- **Respect her privacy.** Even little girls need time to themselves. Your daughter may choose to play

alone in her room from time to time. You can show her that you care and still respect her need for private space.

- **Provide kind, firm discipline and don't be afraid to follow through.** "Wait till your father gets home" doesn't work. Learn effective discipline skills; then be willing to set limits and follow through.
- **Be sensitive about touch, especially in public.** Hugs are wonderful, but sometimes public affection may make your daughter uncomfortable, especially in the later tween years when her friends may tease her if they see her being openly affectionate toward you. Respecting her needs will keep the connection between you relaxed and open.

e! Alert

Encourage your daughter to communicate with you in various ways whether she is upset with you or not. She can scribble you a note when she is mad or sad. This can be her "pass," similar to a bathroom pass her teacher hands out. Use the note over and over as a quick reminder that it is time for both of you to sit down and talk. Vary the talk stations. Talk to your girl at a place and time of her choosing.

Girls need connection with their mothers. Your knowledge of your daughter will help you know when she welcomes a hug and when she does not. It is a delicate balancing act, but time and love will teach you how to stay connected to your daughter at the same time that you encourage her to exercise her independence.

A Friend or a Mother?

"A daughter is a little girl who grows up to be a friend," an unknown author once wrote. That is correct, but a mother is already grown up, so she is the one guiding the relationship. Besides, the relationship between a mother and a daughter should never be an either/or situation, as in "Is my mother my friend or my mother?" You are both. As such, you realize that from the beginning of time, girls have told their mothers when they disagreed with them, "You just don't understand me."

 Alert

Because mothers and daughters are on a different path due to the changing times and the span of years between their ages, they cannot always be best friends, according to Laura Tracy, a family therapist who counsels mother-daughter pairs. Therefore, expect at least a few disagreements to pop up between you and your daughter, just as a matter of course.

Mothers always try to be as understanding and supportive as their daughters' best friends. That is not quite possible because a mother's wisdom and experience overarches the friendly feelings, thereby giving her the ability to sense or see obstacles on the horizon long before her daughter has any inkling. But every woman who has given birth to a daughter has the potential to be both a motherly friend and a friendly mother. Tempered with patience and a willingness to see your daughter's side, you can be a great mom if you just hang in there during your daughter's ups and downs, and offer encouragement whenever needed.

Why Nothing Moms Do Is Right

Sometimes it seems as if nothing you do is right from your daughter's point of view. In this case, just be confident that those days will pass, too. What can help is having a good relationship with yourself, so you do not rise or fall with the emotional roller-coaster ride your daughter will have to take—sooner or later—to grow into the fine young woman she will eventually become.

If you are a mother of a girl who suddenly is very critical of you, realize that she is maturing. While examining some characteristics in you—some of which she may see emerging in herself—she may be surprised. Criticism of a mother is a girl's attempt to find traits to adore and adopt. In a way, this is a flattering development. If she did not care, she would simply overlook you.

BEING HUMAN

Trust that you will make mistakes, and not only as a mother. You are human, and as your daughter changes, so do you. Get out your old yearbooks and prove it. Show her pictures of yourself with bad hair and geeky outfits. Laugh with her over your first dance dress and your first date. Do not be surprised if your daughter acts like a chameleon.

One day she giggles with you and sees your point; the next she gives you that look that disdainfully says, "Mom!" Just remember that you have years of experience as a parent, and it is your job to keep your eyes on the big picture. Sometimes the more volatile your relationship with your daughter is during the teen years, the better it will turn out to be when she is older.

Give her a little extra TLC whenever she makes you feel you cannot please her:

- Put a surprise present—small and just right—on her pillow.
- Give her a funny card with a five-dollar bill for a tiny treat.
- Send a special message to her cell phone. Text her a picture of something she wants with the words: "What else do you want for your birthday?"
- Give her a diary with a big lock and key and tell her to use it to "spill her guts."

Count on this: Confrontations, accusations, and emotional outbursts from your daughter show that you are on the right track. Often it all depends on your and her personality types. Some mothers and daughters show little friction in their relationship. Others have a run-in every other week, but how can you expand your parenting skills if you are not confronted with new challenges?

Think of raising your girl as a most wonderful adventure. Certainly there will be a few or quite a few nerve-racking moments. Otherwise it would not be an adventure.

So assume that the generations will clash now and then at your house, and be ready for it. Call it the pangs of your daughter becoming herself.

NATURE'S BALANCE

One of the hardest things for mothers is to accept their daughters as they truly are because—it seems—that many times the universe is in a joking mood. Many former tomboy moms get real girly girls, and vice versa. Many social-butterfly mothers get daughters who are shy and like to bury their noses in books. This appears to be the result of a generational pendulum that is invisible. A majority of mothers indeed end up with daughters who are their opposites in personality, preferences, and pastimes.

 Question

What do I do if my daughter keeps saying, "I hate you, Mom!"?

If your daughter tells you repeatedly that she hates you, tell her, enough! She does not have to repeat herself. You heard her the first time. When she has calmed down, ask her why she hates you, acknowledge her feelings, and do what you can to mitigate the conflict. Most of all, tell her you love her enough for both of you.

Obviously, nature uses this phenomenon as a way of balancing things. Otherwise, an outdoorsy type of mother would have an even more outdoorsy type of girl, and a girly mom would have an even more girly daughter. In the end, we would have nothing but ultra extremes of daughters, and these developments would be just too predictable. So be thrilled about the girl you are lucky you have. She is just right for you.

A Special Relationship

The more your daughter tests your parenting limits, the more she makes you expand your abilities. You will feel special because you have a special girl. Should there be a moment when you feel like throwing your hands up in frustration because you may see in your daughter the precursors of mistakes you made in your youth, enjoy the moment.

How? By focusing not on the negatives from which your frustration sprang, but by enjoying your daughter more. Remember, a mother is as positively affected by her daughter as the daughter is by her mother. Raising a girl is an important task and benefits you by giving you the chance to experience the following:

- Grow and become a better person because you realize how important setting a good example is.
- Repeat and relive the highlights of your life because you can share your daughter's special occasions, graduations, and award ceremonies.
- Stay young in outlook and even physically because you can experience firsthand the younger generation.
- See a part of yourself immortalized before you pass on because you can count on the fact that some trait—big or small—will emerge in your daughter

and send ripples on to the next generation. Thus, you will live on and on.

For these reasons, make sure your relationship with your daughter is strong. That requires a back-and-forth connection that is vibrant. Discussing the benefits for both parties involved is important.

Bonding Activities

Mothers and daughters can have more fun than any other twosomes because they have a common history, tend to think alike, and may have many similar passions. Find out what your girl gets excited about and share in her excitement. There are so many opportunities for you two to do that. You can discuss with her turning your household "greener" by stepping up your recycling, reusing, and donating efforts. You can go shopping together at the grocery store, the antique shops, and the flea markets. You can stretch, work out, run, or walk the dog together. Afterward you can eat out, or search through the cookbooks and try cooking the most mouthwatering dishes, even some low-cal desserts. You can splurge and head for a day spa for mother-daughter manicures and pedicures, or do housework together until you are ready to drop.

Just ask your daughter what would make her happy and incorporate her wishes into your week, month, or vacation time as much as you can. Zero in on her interests and yours. If they are not compatible, follow your heart's desires as individuals, then meet up and talk about what each of you did, saw, and experienced. Every day work on that wonderful bond you have with your girl. It takes a little effort, but how nice that you have the chance to do it. Therefore, fashion the bond with your best intentions, your best efforts, and the sweat of your brow and your soul. Give your girl all the goodness in you that you can muster.

Girls and Dads

The relationship between a girl and her father is also crucial and deserves to be treated as such. It is most often the first male-female relationship in a girl's life and can form the foundation for how your daughter approaches her future relationships with men. Many men feel awkward dealing with a growing daughter, especially once she reaches the tween and teen years, but your interactions with her are pivotal in her life. From this relationship, your daughter develops a sense of acceptance of herself. Since a child tends to regard herself as others regard her, her father's view is very important. But the father-daughter bond has many more beneficial aspects. If it is strong and healthy, it sends your daughter into the world with clear and healthy expectations for men.

One-on-One Time with Dad

One benefit a daughter gets from relating to her father is a healthy concept of self. According to family therapist Dr. Jane R. Rosen-Grandon, a little girl's self-concept is "largely shaped by this early relationship." Your daughter learns to feel good about being a female child by her interactions with you, as her father. The result is that she feels secure in that role. She reasons that if you respect her as who she is, she must be worthy of that respect and acts accordingly.

Your role as father can only play out if it is allowed to express itself. Therefore, your daughter needs to get as much meaningful time with you as she can from early on. Make it a definite and specific part of her everyday experiences. "Dad time" does not always just happen. It must be scheduled, just like other important things. How do you accomplish this?

- Set aside a special few minutes (or more) every day for your daughter to spend with you and you alone.
- Make sure your daughter has a chance every day to eat at least one meal with you and the rest of the family.
- Be sure to take part in your daughter's bedtime ritual.
- Encourage your daughter to come to you for advice.

Self-Esteem Building via Dad

It is crucial that you help build your daughter's self-esteem. Low self-esteem can undermine your daughter's desire to achieve, affect her negatively throughout life, and may even lead to depression. Even if she turns out to become a high achiever, the question is how much more she could have achieved with her self-esteem at the highest level.

Fortunately, these days the number of fathers trying to do their best by their daughters is increasing even though they may have trouble with the issues of personal relationships.

Play to Your Strengths

By making a deliberate effort, you can build a loving and lasting relationship with your daughter. The decision to commit to making a connection with your daughter is all you need to get started. Your presence and uniqueness will guide you in the right direction. All you have to do is be yourself and be willing to share a part of yourself.

Your strengths can show themselves in many ways, such as:

- If you are inclined to be funny, be goofy with your daughter, play silly games with her, and make her laugh.
- If you like to tell stories, start telling her a tale of adventure—or read one to her—that has many installments, one of which you can narrate to her daily over the course of weeks or months.
- If you are the quiet type, ask your daughter to tell you the names of all her stuffed toys and fill you in on the background of each one.
- If you like to sing, ask her to teach you the songs she learns at school and sing along with her.

Whatever your personality, you can use it to strengthen your bond with your daughter. She will appreciate all your attempts, especially if you establish a pattern in your interactions with her and are reliable and trustworthy, so that she can learn to be reliable and trustworthy, too.

Even if you are a very busy man, make time for your daughter. If you have little free time, you can include your girl whenever you do your chores at home. She can splash in the lawn sprinkler while you do yard work, ride in the wheelbarrow when you transport the raked leaves to the curb, or run to the post office with you. If you are a stay-at-home dad, make sure mom has a special time to spend with the kids, too.

 **Essential**

You should never tell your daughter that she is eating too much or getting fat, even if you are just trying to be helpful. You should not focus on her looks and refer to her physical characteristics. Instead, you should focus on her achievements and praise her for them. Ask her pediatrician if you have health concerns about your child's weight, so that you can learn to talk about healthy eating, instead of dieting, and about getting more physically active.

Perfectionism Is Overrated

Perfectionism is the process of trying to do your best, and still being displeased with the result; it is not a final destination. The word comes from the Latin *perfectus* and means "finished" or "completed," but it does not have to mean "impeccable." That distinction is especially important for girls as they go through school. Too many girls latch on to the idea that whatever they do—from a social studies project to a term paper—has to be flawless. Often that quest for perfection preoccupies them to the exclusion of everything else. Or it can paralyze them and keep them from getting started on an assignment.

Therefore, teach your daughter that perfection in scholastic work is overrated. Nothing should ever be "faultless to a fault." Inform her that you expect her to do well in school, but she should not obsess over each coloring project. Tell her to do all her assignments as well as she can, and then put them out of her mind and go on.

 Fact

If your child gets stressed out, help her do a little work each day before the due date of a project, and get her excited about some other activities, such as some of the extracurricular activities at her school. They will provide a good balance for her.

The best way to lessen the importance of perfection for your daughter is to relax your own standards a little. This is a great time to examine your own behavior. Do you worry too much about every tiny detail at work or at home? If so, schedule a session with yourself about your obsession to be perfect—and let your daughter in on the process. Tell her to remind you when you stress out over trifles.

CHAPTER 10

Boy-Specific Issues

Core gender identity is formed during the toddler years. Children may go through phases, but by age two they should have a conception of themselves as being male. Toddler boys typically identify people's sex by their peripheral characteristics, such as clothing, hairstyle, or use of makeup; they don't have a real conception of what it means to be male. Most modern parents want to avoid raising their children in accordance with old gender stereotypes. They want their sons to be able to express a range of emotions, nurture others, and cooperate as well as compete.

Boys and Emotions

Emotion is vital to human existence, and managing emotions well is a significant part of being healthy and happy. Researchers have believed for some time that emotion (rather than logic) is the driving force in the human brain. Recent studies show that emotion may actually be the link that connects the various functions of the brain and helps them work together. In other words, emotion integrates the different parts of the brain.

 Essential

Emotions are the data you need to make decisions and to stay safe. When you feel lonely, you need companionship. When you are afraid, you need to protect yourself. If you are aware of your emotions and learn to pay attention to them, you will always know what you need to be healthy.

Some researchers tell us that emotion ties together physiological, cognitive, sensory, and social processes, allowing our bodies, thoughts, and senses to work together. Rather than being messy, "sissy" feelings that complicate our lives (best kept private or stuffed away altogether), emotions actually may be responsible for neural integration, keeping us sane, healthy, and functioning effectively. Emotion appears to be the linking force that allows the different parts of our brain to talk to each other.

It is all the more tragic, then, that our culture effectively discourages boys from understanding and feeling their emotions. Numerous writers and researchers, among them Michael Thompson, Dan Kindlon, Terrence Real, William Pollack, and Michael Gurian, have noted the silent crisis that occurs when boys lose the ability to connect with their feelings. Boys are at greater risk for depression, suicide, academic problems, and drug and alcohol abuse than are girls, often because they not only lack the ability to identify their emotions accurately and to learn from them, they actively suppress their feelings. If emotion is intended by nature to keep your son healthy, how can you teach him to understand his feelings, to manage them effectively, and to behave with thoughtfulness and flexibility in a world that does not make a boy's emotional journey easy?

Teaching an Emotional Vocabulary

All too often, boys learn that the ideal man is the strong, silent type. He looks like Arnold Schwarzenegger or Bruce Willis (Clint Eastwood or John Wayne for an older generation) and mutters phrases like "I'll be back," "Make my day," or "Bring it on." Weak men are "girly men." Many boys have exactly two speeds when it comes to emotion: They are *okay*, or they are *angry*. Many parents are shocked at how quickly their sons become belligerent, but it should come as no surprise. Anger is culturally acceptable for boys (and men) and creates its own set of problems. (You will learn more about boys and anger later on.)

In *I Don't Want to Talk about It: Overcoming the Secret Legacy of Male Depression*, psychotherapist Terrence Real talks about the emotional numbing that boys experience as they grow up. They begin life as exuberant, lively little people with a full range of feelings, but by the time they have spent some time in school, they have discovered what *real men* are like and they begin to restrict their expressiveness. Research shows that most males struggle not only to express but to identify their emotions. The formal term for this difficulty is *alexithymia*, and psychologist Ron Levant, EdD, MBA, estimates that as many as 80 percent of men in our society have a mild to severe form of it. If you ask most men what they are feeling, you are likely to hear what they are *thinking* instead. Men (and their sons) often find it difficult to tell the difference. These emotional issues are not the result of differences in the brain; they are most likely differences in what boys and girls learn from parents, peers, and their culture as they grow to maturity.

 Alert

Perhaps the most devastating emotion young boys experience as they grow up is shame. No one enjoys shame, but boys may actually fear it. Shame strikes at a boy's heart; it causes him to close down and to avoid connection with adults at the very time he needs it most. Discipline for your son should never involve humiliation or shame.

Despite the apparent differences in the ways boys and girls, men and women identify and express emotions, most researchers now believe that there is less difference between genders than most people think. For instance, one study found that men and women suffer depression for many of the same reasons and that men are not more likely to be depressed about success and work while women are depressed about relationships. Whether you're a mother or a father, your son is more like you in his emotional wiring than you might suppose.

Building Emotional Literacy

Boys are healthier and happier when they have solid emotional resources and access to all of the varied and intricate parts of themselves. How can parents teach boys to have a rich emotional life, have deep connections to others, and still be full members in the society of men?

To build emotional literacy in your son, you should start by teaching your son an emotional vocabulary. From the time your son is an infant, speak to him with a rich and varied emotional vocabulary. Babies are not born with words for their feelings; they must be taught. You can say, "You look sad" or "You must feel disappointed" without rescuing or pampering your son. You can also talk about your own feelings without making your son responsible for them. When you can say, "I felt scared; did you?" to your boy, you give him permission to feel and to express his own emotions.

Be sure to listen to your son. Then listen some more. One of the best ways to encourage expression is simply to listen without judgment. Show empathy; don't rush to offer solutions. Give your son time to explore his emotions. Remember, you don't have to agree with your son's feelings to listen, nor do you have to accept inappropriate behavior. Listening well is the first step to creating connections and solving problems together.

 **Essential**

You must be sure to model connection and empathy for your son. Mothers and fathers can demonstrate by their own actions what real love and connection look like. When your son lives with respect, love, and empathy, he will find it easier to practice those skills himself.

In addition to listening and teaching your son an emotional vocabulary, make room for your son to be himself. Avoid telling your son what he should or should not feel; give him room to explore his strengths and weaknesses in a safe environment. When your son doesn't need to fear shame or rejection, he can express his emotions, needs, and dreams openly.

Remembering Your Role

Importantly, you should recognize that the outside world (and especially his peers) may toughen up your boy whether you want it to or not; your job is to nurture and encourage him. All boys inevitably learn hard lessons about being "real men." You can best help your son by nurturing his heart and spirit and providing compassion when the world hurts him.

Because boys are sometimes prone to anger and aggression, it is wise to model being calm and respectful when dealing with problems. Take a cool-off if you must, but avoid yelling and anger, and remember that emotions are not mysterious forces that threaten to overwhelm us; they are part of what makes us most human. When you can teach your boy to understand and express his feelings respectfully and clearly, you are helping him take a giant step toward true manhood.

Boys and Anger

For some reason, anger has long been an acceptable emotion in boys and men. After all, the reasoning goes, they have lots of testosterone; they can't help being aggressive. Indeed, anger, including fistfights or other physical confrontations, is often seen as true masculine behavior. Even in these supposedly enlightened times, someone who walks away from a fight may be called a coward.

 Alert

If your son is being bullied, be willing to listen to him and offer him unconditional love and support, and to talk to school staff. Also make sure that your child isn't a bully himself.

Numerous studies have shown that there is no real difference in the way men and women *experience* anger. All people feel anger, and most feel angry about the same things. However, men and women (and boys and girls) *express* their anger in different ways. Men tend to be more physically aggressive, to engage in passive-aggressive behavior more often, and to be more impulsive in expressing anger. Women stay angry longer, are more resentful, and often use relationships as weapons in expressing anger (such as excluding a former friend, starting unpleasant rumors, or insulting someone's appearance).

Some experts believe that boys are prone to anger because it is an emotional substitute for other, less culturally acceptable emotions, such as sadness or loneliness. Parents, too, contribute to boys' anger; research has shown that parents encourage daughters to resolve conflicts peacefully but allow boys to retaliate. Anger is a normal part of the human emotional spectrum; in fact, anger is often what motivates us to solve problems, to stand up for ourselves, and to attempt to right the wrongs of the world. Misdirected anger, however, can cause great harm.

Managing Anger

Everyone gets angry from time to time; your son will, too. How you respond to his anger will teach him about how to recognize and manage it as he grows. First, though, you must learn to deal with your own anger effectively. If you yell, scream, and throw things, your son will, too. Admit your own strong feelings, take a time-out when necessary, and focus on solving problems rather than spreading blame.

You must then teach your son that anger is acceptable, but hurting people or things is not. You can help your son learn that he can feel angry without hurting himself or someone else. Accept his anger and offer him ways to cool down when he needs them. Then, when everyone is calm, sit down and explore ways to make the situation better.

One option you could explore when teaching your son how to deal with anger is to create an anger wheel of choice with your son. Sometime when you are both calm, make a pie chart with suggestions for things he can do when he is angry. (Be sure all of the suggestions are okay with you!) Options might include taking a time-out, listening to music, calling a friend, or shooting hoops in the driveway. Then, when your son is upset, he can look at the wheel of choice for ideas. Having solutions already at hand will help him calm down more quickly.

Finally, learn to listen to your son's real feelings and help him find words to express them. Your son's body language, facial expressions, and gestures will help you know what he is feeling. Gently help him find the right words for his emotions before he reaches the boiling point. Anger is often a smoke screen for other, more difficult feelings such as fear or hurt; when your son can talk about these feelings openly with you, anger may be unnecessary.

Remember, most boys fight, argue, sulk, and suffer. And most boys get up to live and fight another day. Remain calm, remember that feelings are just feelings, and do your best to find solutions to the everyday challenges that life with your son presents.

Boys and Dads

Fathers are different from mothers. They look different, they sound different, they often play in a different way, and they may have a different approach to raising children than a mother does. And that's a good thing. A boy learns from his father, without even realizing he's doing it, what a man is and does. He learns about masculinity, about what men like and don't like. Many adult men report that they either wanted to be just like their dads or wanted to be the exact opposites. Fathers undoubtedly have a powerful influence on their growing sons, and it begins from the moment of birth.

 Fact

Ross Parke, PhD, at the University of California at Riverside, found that fathers are just as good at reading a baby's emotional cues as mothers are, but they respond in different ways. A father's active play and stimulation may actually help a baby learn to be aware of his own internal state and to tolerate a wide range of people and activities.

Early Challenges for Dads

A father's role in the raising of his children has changed dramatically over the past century or two. In previous generations, sons were expected to follow in their fathers' footsteps, apprenticing in their work and in their approaches to life. During the nineteenth century, however, fathers began to go out to work, and the measure of a man's success slowly changed. Rather than the closeness of his family and the strength of his family business, a man's worth could be measured in his income, the value of his house, and the size of his car. Parenting became "women's work"; fathers were just too busy earning a living. And from then on, generations of boys grew up hungering for closeness with a father they barely knew, someone who came home only to eat dinner, look over homework, hear about the day's misbehavior, and watch a little television.

 **Essential**

As boys reach adolescence, their inborn drive to individuate, to become independent people, may lead them to compete and argue with their fathers. Fathers often react by trying to control their sons' opinions and actions, causing conflict. As your boy grows, remember, his task is to become himself and he needs your support and understanding.

Research shows that without a doubt, fathers are an integral part of their sons' healthy emotional, physical, and cognitive growth from their first moments of life. Boys whose fathers love them and can demonstrate that love in consistent, caring ways have fewer problems later in life with peers, academics, and delinquent behavior. One study tracked a group of boys and girls for twenty-six years, exploring the roles of both mothers and fathers in nurturing emotional health and empathy. While the mother's role was important, by far the most influential factor in a child's emotional health was how involved the *father* was in a child's care. In fact, the benefits of having an active, involved father during infancy and early childhood appear to last well into adolescence.

Play and Active Love

Many truly loving dads feel a bit uneasy about showing affection to their young sons. Many moms are usually comfortable hugging and cuddling, but some fathers, who may never have enjoyed an openly loving relationship with their own fathers (and may not be emotionally literate themselves), are hesitant to show affection and warmth in overt, physical ways. Love need not be expressed only in verbal, huggy-kissy ways. There are many ways a father can demonstrate his love for his son, and it's important that he do so as often as possible.

 Fact

It's wonderful to share activities with your boy. Be careful, however, that you don't turn those shared times into unwanted lessons and lectures. Allow your son to learn at his own pace; focus on your relationship with him rather than how well he is performing a certain task. Encouragement and connection will earn you a companion for life.

Spending time together just listening, laughing, and hanging out may be one of the best ways to build a strong bond with your growing son. You can crawl around on the floor with the farm animals and cars when he's a toddler; you can read together, build castles out of blocks, or teach him your favorite sport as he grows. You can wrestle, tickle, bounce, and run.

Of course, for busy fathers with many responsibilities, finding hang-out time can be a challenge. If you consider that your presence in your son's life increases his chances of being successful and happy (and decreases the risk of problem behaviors), you may well decide that there is no higher priority.

 Alert

Sadly, many loving fathers never learn to communicate love in ways their boys can hear and feel. As Dan Kindlon, PhD, and Michael Thompson, PhD, report in *Raising Cain*, ". . . they find it difficult to think in terms of 'love' or to express the love they do feel for a son. Instead, they tend to fall back on what they have been taught to do with other men—namely, compete, control, and criticize."

DADS AND NONVERBAL LOVE

There is another way that fathers can connect and show warmth and caring to their sons, a way that requires no words at all. For example, let's say your son is sad and disappointed because he tried out for a team but was not picked. Sometimes just sitting down next to a somber child without saying a word is enough to encourage the child to open up. If you feel comfortable saying something, offer gentle words like, "I know you're disappointed. But I also know you gave it your best. I know how hard you worked for this." Then just sit quietly together a little while longer. When your son seems to feel a little better, suggest a fun activity the two of you can do together. It'll help take his mind off his disappointment, and you are continuing to show your support.

 Fact

True empathy means understanding the feelings and internal experience of another person; it involves awareness not only of what that person is doing or feeling, but who that person truly is.

Sometimes nonverbal ways of communicating love say far more than the most eloquent words, especially to a boy. Sometimes nonverbal expressions open the door for conversation, understanding, and problem solving. If you pay attention to your own feelings and to those of your son, you will be able to find ways to build powerful connections that can last a lifetime.

Fathers and Empathy

You may be surprised to learn that one of the earliest lessons baby boys learn about empathy comes through active play with their fathers. Experts theorize that being stimulated in this way allows a baby to be aware of both his father's emotional state ("Is he just playing?" "Is he mad?") and his own ("Am I tired of bouncing?" "Is this fun?"). Babies can learn to send signals such as crying or pulling away when they need less stimulation. And throughout a boy's life, his father can be one of his best teachers in the art of empathy and emotional connection.

You can also teach your son unconditional acceptance and understanding. (This is not always easy, especially when your son turns out to have dreams very different from your own.) Another gift is the truth about your own feelings and experience. Remember, you and your son (and all human beings) have mirror neurons that enable you to read another's physical movements, emotions, and nonverbal messages. When you express your feelings clearly, simply, and in nonthreatening ways, your son has the opportunity to learn from your feelings and his own.

Simply put, your son needs calm, clear information about what you think and feel. You can say, "I'm pretty angry at you right now," instead of yelling. You can say, "I'm disappointed because I didn't get the promotion I wanted," instead of stalking off to the garage alone. When you demonstrate emotional honesty and empathy, you offer your son the ability to nurture those qualities himself and to become a stronger, happier man.

How and When to Support Mom

You can support your son by supporting his mother. Many fathers admit feeling a bit jealous of the closeness between a son and his mom, especially during the early years, but parenting is not a competition. (At least, it shouldn't be!) Your son benefits from the relationship he has with each of you. Here are some suggestions for supporting the connection between your boy and his mother:

- **Give your son permission to feel close to his mother and occasionally, to need her.** This may seem obvious, but some men shame their sons for needing a hug or physical comfort from their mothers. Be sure your boy knows that you understand his love for his mother and that you encourage it.
- **Stay actively involved in your son's care, from birth until he leaves your home.** Take time to learn the necessary skills, and then spend as much time as you can caring for your son physically and emotionally. If his mother objects or micromanages your involvement, gently remind her that you, too, are a parent and that your son needs both of you.
- **Support your son's mother when she disciplines your son.** When parents openly disagree about discipline, children learn the fine art of manipulation. Learn all you can about discipline, and then, if you disagree with a discipline decision, talk about it in private and look together for solutions.
- **Treat your son's mother with respect.** Your son will learn how to treat women by watching you. Even when you disagree, make an effort to speak calmly and respectfully. Avoid criticizing his mother to your son.

Boys want to love and feel close to both of their parents. By supporting his relationship with his mother, you will strengthen your son's relationship with you.

Being Your Son's Role Model

Think for a moment about your own father. You may not have known him well; you may not have known him at all. Or you may have years of precious memories. What did your father—or your father's absence—teach you about being a man? About values? About love and family? If your memories of your father are troubling ones, how would you change your own past if you had the chance?

The wonderful thing about raising a son is that it allows you both to share the best parts of your own childhood and, perhaps, to give your son the things you never had.

WORK, MONEY, AND VALUES

Your own choices, actions, and values are the plumb line that your son will use to measure what matters in life. If you work long hours, no matter what your reasons might be, your son will make decisions about work, about family, and about your priorities. If you compete with colleagues, family, and the neighbors to have the biggest house, the nicest boat, and the newest car, your son will decide whether he agrees with you—or not. If you tell your son that you value honesty, but he hears you calling in sick to go skiing or bragging about how you managed to avoid paying taxes, he will make his own decisions about ethics—and about you.

The best way to learn what your son is deciding about life and how to live it is to spend time listening and building a strong connection with him. Children are gifted observers; they rely far more on nonverbal messages than on words. "Do as I say, not as I do" doesn't work with children (especially with teenagers). Remember the list of qualities and character attributes that you want for your son? It's wise to stop occasionally and consider whether or not your own behavior and choices are nurturing those qualities. The good news is that mistakes aren't fatal; they are wonderful opportunities to learn.

DEALING WITH MISTAKES

It is inevitable. Even the most loving and committed parent loses his temper, makes poor choices, or says hurtful, shaming things. No parent enjoys hurting his child, but what truly matters is what you do *after* a blow-up has occurred. Daniel Siegel, MD, puts it this way: "Although ruptures of various sorts may be unavoidable, being aware of them is essential before a parent can restore a collaborative, nurturing connection with the child. This reconnecting process can be called repair . . . Ruptures without repair lead to a deepening sense of disconnection between parent and child."

It is important to notice that your son is not responsible for mending the ruptures in your relationship: Repair always begins with parents. While it may not be easy to admit your own mistakes or to take responsibility for lost tempers and wrong choices, this, too, is part of being a role model for your son. He wants to know that you are capable and competent so that he can believe in his own capability and competence. But he also needs to know that it is okay to admit mistakes, to take personal responsibility, and to say "I was wrong" when it is appropriate to do so. Ruptures can actually make relationships stronger and closer when parent and child—father and son—learn to forgive, find solutions, and reconnect.

Boys and Moms

More than a century ago, Sigmund Freud put into words something that has since become one of the most deeply ingrained tenets of parenting boys. "[A boy's] relationship [with] the mother," he wrote, "is the first and most intense. Therefore, it must be destroyed." Was Freud right? Does it really make a boy "soft" if he is close to his mother? Loving moms must find the balance between nurturing their sons and encouraging independence and confidence.

The Dilemma of Mothers and Sons

Freud was certainly right about one thing: A little boy's relationship with his mother is usually his first experience of intimacy. She may feed him from her breast, rock him to sleep, and appear by his crib when he cries in the night. As he learns to walk, it is usually his mother who provides the safe place from which he ventures out to explore his world and who cuddles him warmly when he returns. It is often Mom who volunteers at school, Mom who plans the birthday parties, and Mom who drives carloads of boys to soccer practice.

Yet when her son approaches adolescence, a mother begins to receive subtle signals that it's time to let go. No more public hugs; touch becomes something that must be carefully monitored. Well-meaning mothers, worried about smothering their growing boys, may withdraw from their sons, leaving them to the world of men and the myths of masculinity. It is a loss—and an unnecessary one—for both mothers and sons.

 **Essential**

> Traditional thinking has attributed boys' delinquent behavior, aggression, even homosexuality, to weak or absent fathers and dominant mothers. Boys, this reasoning says, have to compensate for these overbearing women; they become "too masculine" (or they retreat) in self-defense. Actually, boys benefit from having mothers who are both strong and nurturing—just as they need fathers who are both strong and nurturing.

Boys, too, feel pressure to put some emotional distance between themselves and their mothers. After all, who hasn't heard the dreaded epithets *mama's boy*, *sissy*, and *tied to the apron strings*? As you have learned, American culture places a high premium on self-sufficiency and strength in its males, discouraging emotional awareness and expression. And everyone knows that girls (and moms) are emotional; in order to find a place as a healthy man, the reasoning goes, boys must separate themselves from their mothers.

Raising a son means finding the balance between opposing forces: closeness and distance, support and letting go, kindness and firmness. Mothers can certainly learn how to provide both love and structure and to teach the skills a boy will need to become mature. Love, however, is a necessary part of parenting, and the special bond that many mothers share with their sons is an asset, not a liability. Mothers can teach their boys how to love fully and freely. They offer sons their first lessons in the power of connection.

What Sons Learn from Their Mothers

Boys learn their earliest lessons about love and trust from their mothers. According to William Pollack, PhD, "Far from making boys weaker, the love of a mother can and does actually make boys stronger, emotionally and psychologically. Far from making boys dependent, the base of safety a loving mother can create—a connection that her son can rely on all his life—provides a boy with the courage to explore the outside world. But most important, far from making a boy act in 'girl-like' ways, a loving mother actually plays an integral role in helping a boy develop his masculinity."

Your son will learn self-respect and confidence when you provide a loving and secure home base for him. When you can create a sense of belonging and significance for your boy, teach him life and character skills, and practice kind, firm discipline, he learns to trust, to face challenges, and to move freely into his world. When you take time to listen to him and to focus on solutions to the problems he faces, you teach him emotional awareness and good judgment. A strong and loving relationship with a good mother can help a boy learn the skills of intimacy, support him in developing respect for other women, and prepare him for a satisfying relationship someday.

Connecting with Your Son

The bond between a mother and son often grows out of simply spending time together. From infancy into childhood and adolescence, a good mother is just there. Boys often say that their mom is the one person who understands them. That understanding usually grows out of the hours spent offering undivided attention, responding to signals and cues, and providing comfort, support, and encouragement.

 Fact

Behaviors that make boys different from girls, such as impulsivity, risk-taking, silence, and anger, are often behaviors that mothers struggle with. After all, they didn't do those things when they were kids! Take time to learn all you can about boys, and your boy in particular. Understanding will help you choose your battles and set reasonable limits.

Awareness of your own attitudes toward men and boys will help you connect more easily with your son. Whether you express them openly or not, your beliefs about men will influence your son's feelings about himself. It may be wise to seek out a skilled therapist to help you resolve your own past so that you can build a strong, loving bond with your son.

A boy's bond with his mother is one of the deepest, most enduring relationships he will experience in his lifetime. It should also be one of the healthiest and most supportive.

Here are some suggestions for building a strong, loving connection with your boy:

- **Listen and observe.** Good mothers are willing to spend time just listening and watching. Ask curiosity questions to draw your son out; let him finish his thoughts before offering suggestions or advice.
- **Spend time just being together.** Relationships require time. You must be willing to hang out, to play, and to do things face-to-face with your son. Have at least fifteen minutes a day that belong just to your boy—no multitasking allowed!
- **Respond to your son's cues.** When he says, "I can do it myself, Mom!" teach the necessary skills, be sure he's safe, and then allow him to try. It is skills and experience that build self-esteem.
- **Be curious about his interests.** If your son loves an activity, sharing his enthusiasm is a wonderful way to build connection. Watch his favorite sport with him; admire the new skateboard tricks he learns. Understanding your son's world will keep you connected.
- **Know his friends.** There is no better way to learn about your son than to watch him at play with his friends. As your son grows, welcome his friends into your home. If he can bring his life to you, he is less likely to feel the need to hide it from you.
- **Respect his privacy.** Even little boys need time to themselves. Your son may choose to play alone in his room from time to time, or to disappear into his

computer or stereo headphones. You can show him that you care and still respect his need for private space.

- **Provide kind, firm discipline and don't be afraid to follow through.** "Wait 'till your father gets home" doesn't work. Learn effective discipline skills; then be willing to set limits and follow through.
- **Be sensitive about touch, especially in public.** Hugs are wonderful, but some touch may make your son uncomfortable, especially as he gets older. You may want to have a family rule that bathrooms and bedrooms (yours and his) are private spaces and cannot be entered without knocking. Respecting his needs will keep the connection between you relaxed and open.

Boys need connection with their mothers. If the outside world does not intrude, most are happy to stay close and connected for most of their growing-up years. Your knowledge of your son will help you know when he welcomes a hug and when he does not. It is a delicate balancing act, but time and love will teach you how to stay connected to your boy at the same time that you encourage him to exercise his independence.

Knowing When to Let Go

Even the wisest mother can find it hard to let go in appropriate ways when her son begins to exercise his independence. Your son's desire to do things for himself, from dressing himself to reading his own bedtime story to dating, can feel like a personal rejection. One of the paradoxes of parenting is that if you do your job as a mother well, your son will eventually leave you.

As your son grows, you will learn to find the balance between offering support and stepping back to let him learn from his own experiences—and his own mistakes. Clinging too tightly can create unnecessary power struggles, especially during adolescence (a rather bumpy period for even the closest mothers and sons). Teach skills and listen well and often; then have faith in your son and let go.

 **Essential**

There is a time and place for words; in fact, by using the language of feelings, mothers can help their sons learn to be more comfortable with emotions. Boys will not always want to talk, however, especially when they're hurt or sad. Sometimes, it is the silent spaces in a relationship that speak most clearly.

As your son grows, he will develop new friendships and relationships outside your family. Some of these friendships, especially as he enters adolescence, will not include you—at least, not directly. A wise mom understands that she will not remain number one in her son's life forever.

Boys, Media, and Violence

Boys who are raised with love, who experience belonging and connection, and who learn to identify and manage their emotions rarely have serious problems with violence as they grow up. Yet boys in our society are still more likely to experience harsh discipline, to struggle in school, and to display intense anger. Sadly, the overwhelming majority of violent crimes committed by juveniles are committed by boys.

Why Boys Turn to Violence

Most researchers believe that boys who turn to violence do so because they lack the sense of connection and belonging so critical to emotional health. They may be abused or neglected, or they may have experienced something they find difficult to talk about, such as the divorce of parents, harsh criticism, or constant humiliation. Boys who lack connection with parents are more easily influenced by violence in television, movies, and video games—and more likely to see violence as a solution to their problems.

Violence in the media dulls empathy; children who see screen violence are not likely to comprehend the impact real violence has on real people. After all, Vin Diesel keeps going when he's been shot six times; doesn't everyone?

The Power of Connection

Real relationships remain the best way to prevent violence and to keep your boy healthy and strong. Your son needs your time and attention; he needs to know that he matters and has worth, regardless of his occasional misbehavior. As with so many other aspects of raising a boy, time spent listening, talking, laughing, and just being together will keep you close to your boy and allow you to guide him as he faces life's challenges.

 Alert

> Young children appear to be most vulnerable to the effects of media violence because they learn by imitating, cannot distinguish between reality and fantasy, and are more impressionable than older children. It is especially important to restrict the amount of violence your preschool-age son sees.

Video and Computer Games

Many parents are happy when their boys turn off the TV and turn on a video game. After all, how much harm can a game do? Boys especially enjoy playing together, cheering one another on as they reach different levels and score points. Here's why video games can be problematic: 60 to 90 percent of the most popular video games have violent themes.

There is no question that boys love video games; games appeal to their love of competition and action. Some children, however, report that they have a hard time turning video games off. A 2009 Iowa State University study found that one in ten American children between the ages of eight and eighteen are addicted to video games in much the same way adults can be addicted to alcohol or drugs, and played nearly twice as much as other children. Most of these addicted gamers had sophisticated systems in their bedrooms. Only half of the children in the study had any rules limiting their access to video games.

Boys with strong and loving connections to their families are unlikely to develop problems or mimic the aggressive and often illegal behavior featured in many popular games; some even argue that games increase a child's hand-eye coordination and reflexes. But what about boys on the fringes who lack strong bonds to watchful, caring adults?

No study has ever proved a direct cause-and-effect relationship between violent video games and aggressive behavior. Still, there is lots of evidence to suggest a strong connection. A 2005 review of all available research presented to the American Psychological Association revealed some interesting facts:

- Children who play a violent game for less than ten minutes describe themselves as more aggressive shortly after playing.
- Eighth and ninth graders who spent more time playing violent video games were rated by their teachers as more hostile than other children and more likely to be involved in arguments with authority figures and other students.

- Boys tend to play violent games for a longer period of time than girls, possibly because many games show girls in subordinate roles.
- Children and teens who are most attracted to violent games are also most likely to be vulnerable to the effects of that violence.

Realistically speaking, your son will almost certainly want to own a game system and play video games; if you don't allow it, he will likely play at friends' homes. What should you do to manage the effect of video games on your son?

1. **Pay attention.** Video games have ratings and age limits for a reason. Don't allow your son to play games that are too mature for him.
2. **Watch or play with him.** Look closely at what's in the games he loves; if they are inappropriate or offensive, kindly but firmly tell him they are unacceptable and explain why.
3. **Limit the amount of time your son spends playing video games and watching TV (screen time).** There are far healthier ways he can be using his time and energy.

PART 2

Activities for Your Young Child

CHAPTER 11

Indoor Fun

What do you do when your child is stuck inside all day? Dr. Seuss addressed this problem in one of his best-known stories, *The Cat in the Hat*. The children in this story seemed to be doomed to sit forlornly by the window watching the rain, until the Cat in the Hat comes to entertain. Fortunately, you don't need to juggle fish or fly a kite in the kitchen to turn a gray day into a fun day.

Weather-Related Activities

When bad weather is approaching, you may be facing more of a challenge than entertaining your child. It is common for young children to be frightened of storms. You need to set a good example—if you remain calm and nonchalant, chances are your child will stay calm as well. These activities will keep your child occupied and may even distract him from his anxiety.

You can also talk about other kinds of weather when you're out and about, in the car, or looking out the window in a waiting room or lobby.

Explore the Sensory Aspects
Take your child to a window, porch, or patio and notice in detail what happens with a rainstorm or snowstorm. Talk about the smells, sounds, wind, temperature, and movement. Exciting vocabulary arises out of these times!

Weather Art
Make pictures of a day that is something like the day that is happening. Encourage your toddler to show the elements and someone outside wearing appropriate rain or snow clothing.

Books and Songs
Sort through your child's library and read some stories that have weather as a central theme. *A Snowy Day* by

Ezra Jack Keats would be a good choice. You can sing the following song together:

Rain, rain

Go away

Come again another day.

Rain Sticks

Rain sticks have long been popular as musical instruments in other cultures. Now you don't have to go to a fancy import store at the mall to find them—your child can make one out of materials you have around the house. Many children find the sound of a rain stick to be very soothing. For this activity you will need:

- 1 cardboard paper towel tube or mailing tube
- Crayons
- 2 squares of tinfoil, large enough to cover the ends of the tube
- Masking tape
- 1 long pipe cleaner twisted into a loose coil
- ¼ cup dry rice

1. Let your child color the tube for decoration.
2. Fasten one tinfoil square on the end of the tube with masking tape. Leave the other end open until the tube is filled.
3. Help your child fit the pipe cleaner into the tube. Assist her in pouring in the rice.

4. Close the other end of the tube with the second square of tinfoil. Show your child how to tilt the stick back and forth to create the rain noise.

Shadow Dancing

Here is a great way to get your child moving. Perhaps you can get the whole family to join in. For this activity you will need:

- A light-colored wall
- A bright lamp
- Favorite music

1. Position the lamp in the middle of the room, leaving plenty of space between the lamp and the wall.
2. Turn on the bright lamp and darken the rest of the room. Aim the lamp directly at the wall. Stand your toddler in front of the lamp so that his shadow is cast clearly on the wall.
3. Put on the music and encourage your child to dance so that his shadow dances, too. For a cool-down activity, show your child how to use his hand to create simple shadow puppets.
4. Use your own hands to make shadow animals. With practice, you can make a dog with ears and a barking mouth or a lovely gliding swan. Make up stories about the animal shadows. Your toddler will be enchanted.

Create a Restaurant

Young children love to pretend to cook and eat food. As a bonus, you can reinforce manners and social skills while your child is playing. For this activity you will need:

- Table and chairs
- Paper plates, cups, and napkins
- Plastic tableware
- Poster board
- Crayons
- Notebook
- Plastic or real food
- Play cash register and money

1. Let your child help set up the restaurant. Show her how to set the table.
2. Let your child create a menu on the poster board. You can have her color pictures of the food she wishes to serve. Alternatively, she can paste on magazine pictures.
3. Sit at the table and let your child take your order. Supply her with a small notebook so that she can pretend to write down your order. If desired, let her serve you real or pretend food.
4. Set up a pretend cash register with play money and pretend to pay for the meal, counting out the dollars and cents.

Fact

During rainy days, your toddler will need more exercise to make up for lost time playing outside. Play marching band, do exercises together, or dance to wild music and freeze in place when the music stops. Without enough large muscle activity, you might have a very cranky toddler on your hands.

Play Nurse and Doctor

Many young children are concerned and often fascinated about injury and illness. The subject of doctors and hospitals is something that your child may wish to explore. You can easily change this into a veterinarian theme; simply add a few stuffed animals and a pet carrier. This is a natural way to name parts of the body and describe what hurts. For this activity you will need:

- Doctor's or nurse's hat
- Old adult-sized short-sleeved white shirt
- Fabric marker
- Dolls or action figures (to act as patients)
- Band-Aids
- Gauze or ace bandages
- Rubber gloves
- Plastic syringe

1. Fit the hat onto your child. Make a lab coat by drawing a pocket and adding a name to the shirt.
2. Let your child put Band-Aids on the dolls and pretend to give them shots to make them feel better.
3. Take the stuffed animals to the veterinarian and enjoy questions and answers about what is wrong with each pet.

Play Store

Gather things from around the house and your toddler's room to represent the merchandise for sale. Set the items up on a coffee table for the store display. You can make signs to name the items and list items, or just go with your imagination. Take turns with him, being the customer and being the salesperson. This is a good time to practice questions about price, color, and size. You will be surprised at how fast he picks up your intonation and ways of interacting, as he has heard you do this in all the stores you have visited together. You could create a clothing store, toy store, bookstore, grocery store, or a variety store that has a little of everything.

Play Phone

Your toddler most likely loves to imitate you talking on a cell phone. If she's willing to use a toy cell phone (many toddlers are too sophisticated, insisting on the real phone), set up two phones and encourage her to call anyone she'd like. You can be the other speaker. Don't be surprised if she carries on full conversations, filling in the other person's words.

Make Puppets

Puppets are magical. Not only can they breathe life into any story, but they often seem to have a wonderful effect on young children. Many children who have speech difficulties or are shy often feel more comfortable using puppets for expression. A child can project his own fears, wishes, and dreams through the character of a puppet. Make a puppet with your child and watch his imagination soar.

Rubber Finger Puppets

This a quick and easy way to make finger puppet characters for your child. Cut fingers from rubber gloves could be a choking hazard, so let younger kids draw faces on the fingers of an intact glove. For this activity you will need:

- Old rubber dishwashing gloves
- Scissors
- Permanent markers

Let your child use the markers to create a face and other features on the fingers and palm of the glove.

Paper Plate Puppets

Because this project is so simple, you may wish to let your child make a few puppets and then put on a show. For this activity you will need:

- Dessert-size paper plate
- Crayons
- Wooden craft stick
- White craft glue

1. Let your child decorate the plate with crayons to make a face.
2. Help him glue on the stick to use as a handle.

Sock Puppets

Save the stray socks your laundry seems to create and make puppets out of them. Stitch bits of yarn and scraps of fabric to make the facial features. If you stitch on buttons for the eyes, sew them well, as they are choking hazards for small children. Your toddler can embellish the features with fabric markers. If you want to be really creative, make a whole family of puppets using felt ears, red felt tongues, bow ties, or lace collars. Encourage your child to name the parts. Sock puppets are wonderfully malleable and expressive with the movements of the hand inside the fabric. The little creatures really come to life and evolve into surprising personalities. This is a good way to make language development extremely fun.

For this activity you will need:

- Socks
- Needle and thread
- Scrap pieces of yarn and fabric
- Felt
- Buttons
- Fabric markers

 **Essential**

You can buy a puppet theater from a toy store or toy catalog, or you can make one from a large packing box. Cut it down to a toddler-sized height, cut an opening for the stage window, and attach a curtain made from a piece of fabric. Velcro would work well for this. You are ready for Punch and Judy!

Make a Train

There are many dramatic-play props that you can make with a box. This project is just a suggestion to help spark your own ideas. When cutting the rope, be sure that none of the sections is long enough to be a safety hazard.

For this activity you will need:

- Three or more large boxes
- Lightweight rope, cut into three 1-foot sections
- Scissors
- Tempera paint or markers

- Teddy bears, dolls, or action figures (to act as passengers)
- Engineer's hat
- Small suitcase

1. Arrange boxes to form cars of the train. The front car is the engine. You can designate passenger cars, a dining car, and a sleeping car.
2. Cut a small hole in the front and back sides of each box so that holes in all boxes line up.
3. Connect the boxes with the sections of rope. Knot the rope ends on the inside of each box to secure them. A rope in the front can be used to pull the train.
4. Let your child decorate the train with paint or markers. The train is then ready to carry its passengers.

Playing train can spark conversation about where your toddler might want to go. Who would she like to see who lives far away? What should she take along in a suitcase? If possible, follow up with an actual train ride or take the train ride first.

Make Play Dough

Play dough is universally enjoyable, so why not learn how to make your own? For this activity you will need:

- A saucepan
- ½ cup salt
- 1 cup flour

- 2 tablespoons cream of tartar
- 1 cup cold water
- A few drops of food coloring
- 1 tablespoon of vegetable oil

1. In a saucepan, combine ½ cup salt, 1 cup flour, and 2 tablespoons cream of tartar.
2. Then add 1 cup cold water, a few drops of food coloring, and 1 tablespoon of vegetable oil. Your toddler can help with the measuring, counting, and placing the ingredients into the saucepan. Caution him about the heat of the burner, though. Mix until smooth, and cook over medium heat, stirring frequently.
3. When the mixture sticks to the pan, sticks together firmly, and is no longer slimy to the touch, it's finished. Turn it out onto waxed paper, knead it a dozen times, and let it sit.
4. When the dough is cool, store it in a container with a tight-fitting lid or sealed plastic bags to prevent drying.

Now comes the fun. Sit down with you child and show him how to:

- Roll bits of play dough into a worm or snake.
- Roll a bigger piece into a ball.
- Flatten the ball into a cookie or pancake.
- Pinch off little bits to make peas and put them onto a tiny play-dough plate.
- Prick it with a pen or pencil.
- Slice it with a cheese slicer.

- Cut it with a plastic knife.
- Cut it with cookie cutters.

Supervise carefully to be sure your toddler doesn't try to make a "meal" of the cookies and pancakes.

 **Essential**

Remember that toddlers don't care what they make as long as they get to roll, rub, pat, dab, and draw while they're making it. Adults might care about the finished product; little ones prefer just to putter.

Make an Art Box

Decorate a box and fill it with an assortment of nontoxic supplies:

- Bows and pieces of ribbon
- Coloring book
- Construction paper
- Scraps of foil
- Cotton balls
- Crayons or markers (washable)
- Envelopes
- Glue sticks
- Pipe cleaners
- Paper or old newspaper
- Paper bags, cups, and plates

- Pictures from magazines, greeting cards, and postcards
- Stickers
- Watercolor kit
- Wrapping paper odds and ends
- Yarn and string (16 inches or shorter)
- Pieces of sponge

Older toddlers may also enjoy having their very own easel. Some easels have a dry erase surface on one side or a chalkboard. Look for a child-height tray for paint containers and brushes. Easels are also available in tabletop models.

Pull out the art box on a rainy day! The possibilities are limited only by your imaginations! Younger toddlers can put stickers on paper plates and cups and dab markers onto newspaper. You can cut out the center of a paper plate to make a crown tots can decorate.

Although you often have to curtail your toddler's artistic explorations because they are especially messy, try to accommodate his urge to explore. It's important to accept the fact that your house won't be as tidy as it was before your tot became mobile.

CHAPTER 12

Outdoor Activities

Outdoors is often the best and healthiest place for your child to play and explore. When your child is outdoors, he is less restricted. He is free to use a louder voice, to move around more, and to make more of a mess. Toddlers and the great outdoors are often a perfect match, and going outside is a great way to help toddlers get their recommended sixty minutes of unstructured physical activity each day.

Changing Colors

This is a magical science experiment. Your child can concretely see how plants drink. Simply fill a clear glass with water. Add enough food coloring to distinctly color the water. Cut a celery stalk and place it in the glass. See how long it takes for the celery to take on the color of the water.

Pressed Flowers

You will be surprised how easy it is to get a nice result from pressing flowers. Arrange the blossoms between layers of newspaper or waxed paper. Press them under wooden blocks or between the pages of a large book.

Bugs!

You may be wrinkling your nose in disgust, but the fact is most children are fascinated with insects. Toddlers are naturally curious and often don't become afraid of insects unless they are imitating the reactions of someone else. There are certainly more insects on this planet than any other species, and they are just about everywhere. Don't ignore them. Capitalize on your child's interests in learning.

Bigger Bugs

Simply provide your child with a magnifying glass and some time to observe the insects all around her!

Fingerprint Bugs

These personalized insects will help your child develop creativity and fine motor skills. Pour some tempura paint into a pie tin. Have your child dip her thumb into the paint. Help her press her thumb onto the paper to create a thumbprint. She can use crayons to add the head, legs, and antennae.

Snow Pictures

Your child will enjoy livening up the yard with these beautiful but temporary creations. Half the fun is watching what happens when the snow starts to melt. Thin some tempura paint with water, and fill spray bottles. Let your child spray the paint onto the snow to create any pictures he wishes.

Cloud Watching

This classic activity is still one of the best ways to spend an afternoon. What a great way to spend some quiet and quality time with your young child! Find a nice clear area where you and your child can lie down and watch the clouds. Be sure to encourage your toddler to use her imagination. Does she see animals, people, different shapes?

Ring Toss

This variation on the classic is designed for young children. It lets all players feel successful. All you need to do is place a hula hoop on the ground in a flat area. Designate a place for each player to stand. The younger the child, the closer he should be to the hula hoop. Show your child how to toss the beanbag, and encourage him to get it inside the hula hoop. If he is having a lot of difficulty, you can move him closer to the ring.

Pinecone Bird Feeder

Not only will your toddler enjoy making this project, but the finished bird feeder will attract birds for your toddler to watch and enjoy! Here's what to do:

1. Attach a 12-inch length of yarn or twine to a pinecone. Make a loop at the loose end for hanging the bird feeder.
2. Help your toddler spread peanut butter on the pinecone.
3. Pour birdseed into a bowl. Show your child how to roll the coated pinecone in the seeds to coat it.
4. Take your bird feeder outside, and hang it where your child will be able to watch the visiting birds.

Magic Sun Prints

This activity seems to work like magic. This is a fun way to explore the sun's power as well as shadows and shapes.

1. Ask your child to help you find objects to use to make silhouettes. Flat objects work best. Some good examples include keys, erasers, forks, and shoelaces.
2. Go outside on a sunny day. Have your toddler arrange the chosen objects on dark construction paper.
3. Leave the paper out in full sunlight for a few hours. The sun will fade the exposed paper to a lighter shade than the paper protected by the selected objects.
4. Remove the objects to reveal the silhouette design.

Roadway

This activity combines the fun of sensory play with your child's imagination. It works great in any outdoor dirt or sand area. Simply show your child how to use a spatula to draw roads and passageways in the sand. Then let her create the roadways and then drive vehicles around.

Glacier Creatures

This is a good opportunity to talk about temperature and melting. Be sure to choose toys that are not a choking hazard. Start the activity the night before a warm day when you're likely to be outside at a water table or in a play pool.

First, place a toy(s) in a plastic container(s) (small reusable plastic containers work great). Fill the container with water and freeze. When the "glacier" is frozen, remove from the mold and add to your child's warm play water.

Mud Paint

It's okay for young children to get dirty when they play. Why not? That's why you do this activity outside! Here's what to do:

1. Either find some mud outside for your child to use, or help him make some mud by adding water to dirt. Use a spoon to whip the mud up to a creamy consistency. Add more water if needed.
2. With the spoon, place a blob of mud on the poster board for your child to finger paint with.

Make Homemade Bubble Solution

Save money and have fun at the same time. You can make as much bubble solution as you need when you need it. Just adjust the proportions to make the amount of solution you desire.

The recipe is simple: Mix together ½ cup liquid dish soap, 2 tablespoons glycerin or light corn syrup, and

5 cups water. Don't be afraid to alter the proportions and experiment to create the perfect bubble solution.

Bubble Catch

Here is a fun and cooperative game that you can play with your young child. The best part is that you will have pretty pictures when you are done. Here's what you'll need:

- 2 small containers of bubble solution with bubble wands
- Food coloring or tempera paint
- 2 sheets light-colored construction paper or poster board

1. Add 1 or 2 drops of food coloring or paint to each container of bubble solution.
2. Let your child gently blow bubbles toward you. Hold out the sheet of paper to catch the bubbles. Take turns blowing and catching the bubbles.
3. When you are done, each player will have a picture of the bubble residue.

CHAPTER 13

Brainy Fun

Your young child learns best through play. This is her way of exploring and learning about her environment. For example, when your child is playing with Legos, she is learning about colors, counting, and spatial relationships. You can help promote your child's mastery of basic concepts with some of these fun, hands-on activities.

Language and Literacy

Language development is related to a lively approach to the world through the senses. What can you do to enrich your toddler's sensory experience?

- Go to an art museum and look at the large paintings and sculptures. Talk about color, shape, and size.
- Vary the music you and your child listen to. You don't need to be limited to children's songs, but your child shouldn't always have to listen to classic rock either. Cover a wide repertoire of classical, blues, world music, rock and roll, jazz, punk, alternative, and country music and have fun describing it with vocabulary connected to sound—fast, slow, loud, soft, smooth, happy, sad—and have fun dancing around the room to express the mood of the music.
- Get out the karaoke machine and ham it up. You may be surprised at how your little one naturally uses a microphone and belts out a pretty good tune.
- Explore the language of touch. Look for things around the house that are furry, soft, hard, smooth, warm, cool, or rough. This discussion could include the shapes of items as well and questions such as, "Where is the smooth red ball?" "Can you bring me the cool ice cube?"

Head Out for a Chat

Toddlers love to go out and about—and outings create even more things to talk about. Go to the zoo and watch all the animals. Reinforce with books about the animals after you are back home. A trip to an ice cream parlor is rich with opportunity, not just calories. Let your child decide what flavor of ice cream she would like, how many scoops, and whether in a cone or a cup. Will she need a few napkins? How about a spoon? Where should we sit? All these discussions are real to the child. "Oops! The ice cream is melting and dripping. Now Mommy's ice cream is melting and dripping." The repetition makes an impression on the child and very soon you will hear those words being spoken, and almost always in the correct context. The human brain is amazingly sensitive and organized, like a fantastic computer. You will see it in action, as your child adds vocabulary by leaps and bounds.

Library Story Time

Most public libraries have a toddler story time. This makes a marvelous outing and creates a lot to talk about. It's a chance for you to meet other parents and socialize a bit. With weekly story times you will probably make friends among the others in the book circle. Have some fun selecting just the right chair or pillow to sit on and getting some books to take home afterward. Children's librarians are a good source of information about specific books for particular ages of children. You may find that in your community the bookstores also offer story times for toddlers.

Fine-Tuning Listening

Seize opportunities to encourage your toddler to tune in to the world of sound. For example, when you're in the car, point out the shriek of a police siren, the blare of a horn, or the whistle of a train. When you go for a walk around the neighborhood, instead of plugging in your earbuds, talk with your toddler about the tweet of a bird, the rustle of leaves, or the whoosh of the wind.

 Fact

Appropriateness is everything when it comes to activities for toddlers. You need to be familiar with what toddlers can and cannot do, what they enjoy, and what may frustrate them. You probably know better than to purchase a chemistry kit for your two-year-old or to ask your three-year-old to join you in a game of Gin Rummy.

In the house, listen together to the crackle of a fire, the hiss of a kettle, or the ring of a kitchen timer. Use your voice as well; hum, whistle, and sing to your little one. She won't care if you can't carry a tune.

Careful listening helps toddlers to reproduce the sounds needed for speech today, to recognize the subtle differences in sound needed for speaking tomorrow, and to sound out words when they're learning to read in the years to come.

Letters

Help your child with letter recognition and awareness. Show her how there are letters all around her. For example, have your child pick out and identify letters in her alphabet soup or cereal. For a variation, give your child some dry alphabet cereal or noodles and challenge her to find certain letters. Perhaps you can help her spell her name.

Shapes

When your child is learning about shapes, he is learning about basic mathematical and spatial concepts. Everything has a shape. Start to broaden your child's awareness by pointing out the shapes of everyday objects.

Shape Hunt

From some construction paper, cut out a circle, a square, and a triangle. Work with one shape at a time. Show your child the shape, and tell him that he is going on a shape hunt. Help him find other items that are that shape. For example, show him the circle and then go around the room looking for circles. Help him find circles in things like a doorknob, a plate, or a clock.

Shape Characters

From some construction paper, cut out a circle, a square, and a triangle. Let your child color in facial features for each shape. Then, teach your child the following rhymes for each shape:

I am Suzy Circle, watch me bend

Round and round from end to end.

Tommy Triangle is the name for me,

Count my sides; one, two, three.

Sammy Square is my name;

My four sides are all the same.

Colors

There are many activities that can help your child learn color identification. The most successful activities are hands-on and engage your child's senses. Here are just a few to get you started.

Color Lotto

Lotto games are an excellent way to help your child enhance her memory and problem-solving skills. You can adapt this game for shape, letter, or number recognition as well. Simply make two lotto cards for each color by cutting an index card in half crosswise. Cut pieces of colored construction paper to fit the halves of each card. Have your child help glue the paper on the cards. Each card should have a colored side and a blank side. Mix the cards up and then arrange them in rows colored side down.

Your child is to flip over two cards and try to find a match. When she does, she can remove the cards from the layout. If she does not make a match, she is to turn the cards back over and try again. Do not worry about strictly following the rules. Your child may need to turn over more than two cards or even keep them facing up.

Squish and Mix

This is a great sensory activity that will help your child observe what happens when colors are mixed. Be sure to talk to your child about what she sees.

Add a small amount of the blue and red paints in a zip-close bag and seal. Place that bag inside a second bag and seal. Let your child squish and knead the bag to mix the paints and create the color purple. Repeat with other color combinations.

Numbers

Children develop a mathematical awareness at an early age. Although your toddler is not ready for mathematical equations, you can start to introduce him to the concepts of quantity and the symbolic representation of quantity.

Yarn Numbers

Show your child how to arrange pieces of yarn to make the shapes of different numbers. You can adapt this activity to teach letters and shapes as well.

Number Bags

Here is a fun activity that will reinforce number concepts and counting skills. Mark several paper bags with a number, starting simply with just 1, 2, and 3. Take your child outdoors or around the house to find things to collect, such as leaves or small racecars. Direct him to put the appropriate number of items in each bag.

CHAPTER 14

Holidays and Parties

Holidays are special times when ordinary routines are broken and there are new foods, visitors, and activities, and the excitement can be overwhelming for young children. Although you want a holiday to be fun for your young child, remember that she may need some quiet one-on-one time with you. Take some time out of your hectic schedule to try one of these activities with her.

Birthday Parties

A toddler does not have a clear sense of time, particularly in the large sense of a year. It can be fun, however, to add festive touches of decorations, food, and creative activities to a child's party. Invite just a few friends, and keep everything simple. The best way to plan for a successful children's party is to lower your expectations. Toddlers are easily impressed, so you don't need to hire the most popular performer around and a cast of thousands to entertain your guests. Invite only a few of your child's playmates, and keep the party short and simple. Refreshments, gift opening, and two or three simple activities would be plenty. Remember that the party is for your child and his friends, not for you.

By about age two, children are old enough to understand and get excited about the prospect of having relatives and friends over, receiving presents, and eating cake and ice cream for "Me birthday party!" To help make your child's party a success, keep these tips in mind:

1. Include your toddler in the planning, having him help select the refreshments and the theme.
2. Keep in mind that clowns or mask-wearing magicians could scare a toddler.
3. Keep it short, at around two hours. The anticipation beforehand and the excitement of the party itself are apt to fray your child's nerves—not to mention yours!

4. Ask other parents to stay with their children for the duration of the party. It's hard for one parent to supervise a group and keep everyone safe.

5. Consider having your child open presents after the guests leave so they don't get upset about wanting presents, too.

6. Provide party favors to help everyone feel included.

New Year

Your child will enjoy making noise and helping to celebrate the new year without having to stay up until midnight. You might make a noisemaker and wear a funny hat to celebrate the coming of the new year. Explain in a simple way that a new time is beginning. The child will not understand complex descriptions of the calendar and time, and will probably fall asleep before midnight.

Valentine's Day

Love is in the air! Your toddler is just starting to learn about love and relationships. At this stage in her life, your toddler's greatest love is probably you. But soon, her social world will be expanding. Talk about love and caring while you make paper cards to give to friends and family.

Valentine's Day is a great chance to reinforce recognition of the colors pink and red, too. It's also a good time to talk about shapes and sizes. Cut out hearts in different sizes and colors and let her glue them onto cards.

St. Patrick's Day

It is said that anyone can be Irish on St. Patrick's Day. Focus on the color green and share some of the legends and lore of this holiday with your child. You can enjoy stories about elves, leprechauns, and fairies, and note the fun of everyone wearing green. This is a good time to talk about rainbows and the colors in the rainbow.

Easter

There are many symbols and traditions associated with this holiday. Easter eggs and the Easter Bunny may be the two most familiar to young children. Here are some simple activities that your toddler is sure to enjoy.

- **Your toddler will likely be enthusiastic about making and talking about bunnies.** You can use cotton balls to decorate a paper bunny's tail.
- **Coloring eggs is always a big hit.** Natural dyes are interesting to try. Onion skins or beets make very nice colors. Brewed black tea makes a warm, delicate brown. When you use natural dyes, you may need to soak the eggs in the dyes overnight, remembering that the longer you dye, the darker and brighter the color.
- **A toddler is mature enough to hunt for slightly hidden Easter eggs.** You can tuck the eggs around the house so that a piece of each one shows, making it easy and fun for the toddler to find the treasures.

Fourth of July

Your toddler is too young to understand the full history behind this holiday. Keep it simple, and explain that you are celebrating the country's birthday. Your child will love being a part of the festivities. The Fourth of July is a great opportunity to talk about the flag's colors of red, white, and blue. If your town has a parade, that can be exciting for a toddler. Who can resist the rhythm of majorettes and marching bands? It can be an opportunity afterward to experiment with marching and imitations of the various band instruments.

Halloween

The older toddler may enjoy arts and crafts activities associated with Halloween—finding a pumpkin, watching an adult carve a face, cleaning out the seeds and perhaps roasting them in the oven for a fall snack. Your toddler can make a spider out of a paper plate with some glued-on legs. Young children enjoy costumes, but be careful to not let the child become overstimulated with trick-or-treating and too much candy.

Thanksgiving

The history of this holiday is more than your child can understand. Discussions about Pilgrims and Native Americans are not relevant to your child's experience of the world around him. The turkey, on the other hand, is a concrete symbol of the Thanksgiving meal. You may also choose to have a discussion about abundance and thankfulness during this holiday. Your child might enjoy being a part of Thanksgiving shopping and meal preparation, learning about particular foods—cranberries, pumpkin, stuffing, and turkey. The concept of gratitude is a bit abstract, but you can weave it into the preparations for the day.

Your older toddler can help set the table, an important job and a chance to practice naming the utensils, counting them, and talking about positions of items.

Chanukah

Chanukah is a holiday steeped in traditions. Don't forget to share some of your favorite ways to celebrate with your young child. This holiday lasts for eight days. Here are two favorite activities to get you started with the celebration.

Handprint Menorah

This activity is a great way to reinforce holiday traditions as well as introduce your child to counting concepts.

1. Pour blue and yellow paint into separate pie tins. Have your child dip her hands in the blue paint and then press them flat onto construction paper. Her thumbs should overlap while her fingers should be spread apart.
2. Show her how the print resembles a menorah, with the thumbprints representing the Shamash. Count the eight candles with her.

3. Wash your child's hands. Then have her dip one finger into the yellow paint. Help her press her finger over each candlestick to make a flame.

Dreidel, Dreidel

Your toddler will enjoy spinning her body like a dreidel. The song can be sung to the traditional dreidel tune or to "Row Row Row Your Boat." Teach your child the following song and then have her spin around while she sings it:

Dreidel, dreidel, dreidel,

I'm spinning all around.

Going slow and going fast

Until I'm on the ground.

Christmas

Even your young toddler will be aware of the hustle and bustle of the Christmas season. It is hard to shelter him from the music, the commercials, the movies, the decorations, and everything else. He does not have to be a passive bystander, though. These activities will encourage him to contribute festive decorations for your home. The shopping and meal preparation make great times for learning new words.

Your toddler can help to decorate the Christmas tree, naming each item as it is placed on a branch. You and he can make colorful items to put on the tree—ornaments or chains. Some families keep these little treasures for years, remembering the toddler's second or third Christmas again and again.

Handprint Wreath

This is a personalized holiday decoration. You may wish to do one with each member of your family. You'll need a paper plate, scissors, green and red construction paper, a pencil, and craft glue. Here's what to do:

1. Cut the flat center out of the paper plate so that only the rim remains.
2. Have your child spread his fingers and lay his hand flat on the green construction paper. Trace around your child's hand with the pencil to create a hand template.
3. Cut out a dozen hands from the template.
4. Cut out three red circles, about the size of a grape.
5. Help your child arrange the hands around the plate ring. You want the hands to overlap and the fingers to reach outward.
6. Help your child glue the hands to the plate. Let him glue on the red "berries" for a finishing touch.

Kwanzaa

Kwanzaa is a relatively new holiday, honoring the heritage and history of African Americans. It could be a simple way to introduce your child to the traditional colors of Kwanzaa.

Kwanzaa Placemat (Mkeka)

This is a personalized holiday decoration. You may wish to do one with each member of your family. Here's what to do:

1. Fold a piece of black construction paper in half crosswise.
2. Cut slits from the folded center to about 1 inch away from the edge. Space the slits 1 inch apart. Unfold the paper.
3. Cut out strips of red and green construction paper just a little thinner than 1 inch and as long as the black paper.
4. Help your child weave the strips through the black paper. Alternate the red and green strips and be sure to push each one snug against the previous one. Don't worry if the pattern is not perfect.
5. Secure any loose ends with tape.

Recipes to Cook for and with Your Child

A Little Chef

Your toddler will love to cook with you! Everyone loves to eat, and getting food ready to eat is a purposeful kind of play. Involving little ones in food preparation creates the kind of pride of accomplishment that can bring about a willingness to eat their creations. Pull up a chair or step-stool so youngsters can join you at the counter. Enlist their help with a variety of food preparation chores by giving very young toddlers directions for one simple task at a time and giving a hands-on demonstration. Toddlers as young as fifteen months should be able to help with a number of chores, such as:

- **Setting time on a digital timer.** This is a good chance to practice numbers and counting.
- **Scrubbing fruits and vegetables.** Since a simple rinse in water is all that's required, this is an easy one for toddlers.
- **Pouring water.** Let them pour water 1 cup at a time into the pot that will be used for boiling pasta, rice, eggs, vegetables, or cooked cereal. Have fun counting. Keep them away from the stove, and let them work with cold to lukewarm water only!
- **Spreading.** Let them use a plastic knife to spread peanut butter or cream cheese on celery sticks.
- **Making omelets.** Let them sprinkle shredded cheese onto the eggs; the eggs and pan must be cool.
- **Cutting cookies.** Put each ingredient for the cookie recipe into a separate bowl. Help toddlers pour

them all into one bowl, stir, roll out the dough, and cut it with cookie cutters.

- **Stirring juices.** After you pour the thawed juice into the pitcher of water, have your toddler stir. Teach him to stir gently, but use a big pitcher so there's room to slosh!

- **Cleaning the counter.** Toddlers can wipe down the counter with a damp dishrag or sponge. (Not that you'll end up with a clean counter for the first few years of practice, but focus on the participation, not the result.)

- **Setting the table.** Keep the directions simple! First instruct them to put a fork by each plate. When they are finished, they can do the spoons, and then the bread knives. They can also put out the butter, ketchup, salt and pepper, and napkins, too, if they're given one item to do at a time.

Cooking develops math skills (counting and measuring), nutrition, and science concepts (prediction, cause and effect). Cooking is even more fun if you make a large picture of your favorite dish on poster board. Use cutout shapes of cups and spoons showing the number needed in the recipe.

The Recipes

Here are 50 delicious, easy recipes you can make for or with your toddler. Some are great as meals or parts of a meal, and others work well for snacks, either at home or on the go.

The recipes marked with an asterisk (*) are suitable for trying *with* your toddler.

GREAT FOR MEALS

GREAT FOR SNACKS

Great for Meals
Steamed Grapes and Squash*

Have you ever tried cooking grapes? They add a great taste when paired with butternut squash. Steaming grapes makes them more tender and less of a choking hazard. In addition, you don't need to peel them. You should still supervise your child closely when eating any kind of grapes.

YIELDS 5 SERVINGS
1 medium butternut squash
15–20 large, seedless green grapes

1. Wash the squash. Peel, remove the seeds, and cut into 1-inch cubes.
2. Place the squash in a steamer basket. Place in a pot over about 2 inches of water. Bring to a boil and steam for about 6 minutes.
3. Wash the grapes. Cut in half, if desired.
4. Add the grapes to the steamer basket and steam for another 6 minutes, or until tender when pricked with a fork.
5. Serve in pieces, or mash to desired consistency.

Scrambled Eggs with Cheese

Use a mild cheese in this recipe, especially if your toddler hasn't had a wide variety of cheeses yet. Mozzarella melts particularly well, as does Monterey jack or a mild Cheddar. Avoid sharp cheeses until your toddler is more used to them.

YIELDS 1 SERVING
1 egg
1 tablespoon milk (regular or soy)
2 tablespoons grated cheese

1. Crack the egg into a bowl and add the milk. Beat thoroughly.
2. Pour the egg into a medium-hot nonstick frying pan, adding a bit of oil or butter if the egg starts to stick.
3. Scramble the egg, adding the cheese about halfway through. Continue scrambling until the egg is cooked and cheese melted.

Simple French Toast

Once your little one has mastered simple French toast, try adding fruit to make it a bit more appealing to the rest of the family. Mix a few mashed blueberries or strawberries into the egg mixture, for example. Or, if you want to try a creamier French toast, add a little applesauce to the egg mixture. You can also add a little vanilla or almond extract.

YIELDS 3 SERVINGS
1 egg
1 tablespoon milk or water
1 teaspoon white sugar
Pinch of cinnamon
1 tablespoon oil
3 slices whole-wheat bread

1. Combine the egg, milk, sugar, and cinnamon in a medium bowl. Beat thoroughly.
2. Heat the oil in a large frying pan. One at a time, dip the bread slices into the egg mixture and soak for about 10 seconds. Flip the bread over and soak on the other side.
3. Place each of the bread slices into the heated pan.
4. Fry on each side until lightly browned, usually 1–3 minutes per side.
5. Let cool completely before cutting into pieces and serving as finger food.

Noodles with Cheese

Experiment with conchiglie (shells), farfalle (bow ties), fusilli (twists), rotelle (wagon wheels), or any other fun pasta shape your child might like. For basic macaroni and cheese, try using Cheddar, Colby, or Monterey jack cheese. Don't rinse pasta before serving to your toddler. The starch in the cooking water will make the pasta a little bit sticky, which is perfect for young fingers.

YIELDS 3 SERVINGS
4 cups water
¾ cup elbow macaroni (or other shape)
2 tablespoons butter
2 tablespoons all-purpose flour
1½ cups milk
¾ cup grated cheese

1. Bring the water to a rapid boil in a large saucepan.
2. Add the macaroni, stirring to break up the pasta. Cook for 12–15 minutes, or until noodles are completely tender. Drain.
3. In a small saucepan, melt the butter over low heat. Stir in the flour, whisking constantly until it's dissolved. Add milk and cheese, stirring constantly, until it thickens into a sauce.
4. Pour the cheese sauce into the noodles, tossing to mix.
5. Allow to cool before serving to your toddler.

Dried Bean Stew

A variation on Indian dhal recipes, bean stew allows for more variety. Aside from chickpeas and kidney beans, there are fava beans, split peas, great northern beans, mung beans, pinto beans, soybeans, and many more varieties. Any sort of meat can be substituted for the ham, and of course the meat can be omitted entirely for vegetarian families.

YIELDS 4 SERVINGS
¼ cup dried lima beans
¼ cup dried black beans
4 cups water
1 small potato
½ cup tomato sauce
½ cup ham, diced

1. Wash the dried beans. Place in a large saucepan with enough water to cover them. Soak overnight in the refrigerator.
2. In the morning, drain the soaking water and refill with fresh water, about 3 inches over the top of the beans. Bring to a boil; then simmer for about 1 hour.
3. Wash and peel the potato. Dice into small pieces; then add to the cooking pot.
4. Add in the tomato sauce and ham. Continue simmering until potatoes are cooked, about another 45 minutes.
5. Allow to cool; then fork-mash before serving.

Broccoli with Oranges and Almonds*

A great way to serve vegetables: mix them with sweet fruit! Even fussy eaters will find something they like in this broccoli dish, which combines fruit with broccoli and nuts.

YIELDS 3 SERVINGS
½ head broccoli
2 tablespoons butter
¼ cup sliced almonds
4 cups water
½ orange

1. Wash the broccoli and remove the stem. Dice into small florets.
2. Heat the butter in a medium saucepan. Toast the almonds for about 5 minutes, or until lightly browned.
3. Bring the water to a boil. Add the broccoli and cook for about 15 minutes, or until the broccoli is tender.
4. Slice the orange in half and remove the fruit with a grapefruit spoon. Cut into small pieces. Toss the cooked broccoli, almonds, and oranges together.
5. If the textures are too challenging, omit the almonds and purée the broccoli and orange, adding milk as necessary to thin the mixture.

Fish Chowder with Corn

Chowder is a type of thick, creamy soup that usually contains seafood and/or potatoes. The starch from the potatoes binds the soup into a stew, and the resulting smooth texture is great for young eaters. If fork-mashing leaves too many discrete pieces, purée in the food processor before serving.

YIELDS 2 SERVINGS
½ medium white potato, diced
⅛ cup corn
⅛ cup peas
2 cups water
1 small whitefish fillet
1 tablespoon butter
¼ cup milk (regular or soy)

1. Combine the potato, corn, and peas in a saucepan with the water. Bring to a boil, then cook for 25 minutes, or until the potatoes are soft.
2. Wash the fish fillet, removing all bones. Place the fish into the bottom of a microwave-safe dish and add enough water to cover the bottom of the dish. Cover with either a lid or microwave-safe plastic wrap.
3. Cook the fish in the microwave on high for 3 minutes. Let rest, then cook for another 3–4 minutes. Fish is done when it flakes easily with a fork and is an opaque color.
4. Drain the vegetables. Add the fish, butter, and milk, stirring over low heat until the chowder thickens. Allow to cool, then fork-mash or purée before serving.

Baked Zucchini

Baking zucchini with tomato sauce and cheese is almost like giving your toddler pizza—but a healthier one that's also lower in fat. Add salt and pepper for older kids.

YIELDS 2 SERVINGS
1 medium zucchini
½ cup tomato sauce
½ cup shredded mozzarella
1 tablespoon oil

1. Preheat the oven to 350°F. Scrub the zucchini and trim both ends. Slice into rings.
2. Place the zucchini into a baking dish. Smother with the tomato sauce and mozzarella and oil, then cover the dish.
3. Bake for 45 minutes, or until the zucchini is very soft and the cheese is melted. Serve as is or fork-mash if desired.

Bell Pepper Faces*

Here's a fun way to encourage your toddler to eat vegetables. Go for contrasting colors; reds, greens, and oranges will stand out nicely against a white or yellow tortilla. It doesn't matter if your tot's meal looks like a Rembrandt painting, but he'll be more excited about it if it's colorful.

YIELDS 1 SERVING
1 flour or corn tortilla
1 cherry tomato
¼ green pepper
1 slice cheese
½ carrot
1 tablespoon peanut butter

1. Place the tortilla on a flat plate. Slice the cherry tomato in half. Place on the tortilla for eyes.
2. Slice the bell pepper in half and remove all seeds. Cut 5–10 thin strips; place at the top of the tortilla for hair.
3. Cut the cheese into 2 half-circles. Place at the sides of the tortilla for ears.
4. Wash and peel the carrot. Grate several pieces and place on the tortilla for the mouth and eyebrows.
5. When the vegetables are all positioned the way you like them, affix each to the tortilla with a dab of peanut butter.

Leafy Greens with Almonds

This is a fun recipe that uses lots of spinach. Leafy green vegetables are some of the most beneficial ones out there. Most toddlers need little encouragement if they've been offered such vegetables from a young age. Almonds add a pleasant crunch, but don't substitute walnuts or peanuts; those nuts are larger and chunkier, and not safe for young children.

YIELDS 1 SERVING
1 cup fresh leafy greens
2 cups water
2 tablespoons butter or margarine
2 tablespoons sliced almonds

1. Wash the green leaves thoroughly, removing any damaged parts.
2. Steam in a small amount of water for about 10 minutes, or until the vegetables turn a bright green color.
3. Melt the butter in a small frying pan. Toast the almonds for about 5 minutes, stirring constantly to prevent burning.
4. When the almonds are toasted, mix with the cooked greens. Fork-mash if desired.

Best Baked Potatoes

If you don't have 1 hour to bake a potato in the oven, don't despair. They can also be cooked in the microwave with little sacrifice in flavor. Follow the same washing and pricking instructions; then cook on high for 5 minutes. Turn the potato over and cook for another 4–5 minutes. If the potato middle isn't soft, cook for another 1–2 minutes and recheck.

YIELDS 2 SERVINGS
1 medium russet potato
½ tablespoon oil

1. Preheat the oven to 350°F.
2. Scrub the potato thoroughly with a vegetable brush. Cut out any bad spots.
3. Pat the potato dry with a paper towel; then poke 8–10 holes into the potato, using a fork or other sharp implement.
4. Pour the oil into a paper towel and rub it around the potato. Place on a baking sheet and bake for 1 hour, or until the potato skin is crispy.
5. When cooled, cut the potato in half. Scoop out the potato from the skin, and fork-mash if desired.

Baked Sweet Potatoes*

There are a variety of different kinds of sweet potatoes. Yams have a bright orange interior and a sweet taste and soft texture. True sweet potatoes are lighter and firmer. If your baked potatoes come out too dry, it's probably due to a combination of factors, starting with temperature. Cooking potatoes at 400°F makes the outside cook faster than the inside, leaving you with a burned skin and a hard, dry, under-cooked middle. Also, look at the type of potato; yellow-fleshed potatoes tend to be drier than their white-fleshed cousins.

YIELDS 2 SERVINGS
1 medium sweet potato or yam

1. Scrub the sweet potato thoroughly with a vegetable brush. Cut out any bad spots. Poke 8–10 holes into the potato, using a fork or other sharp implement.
2. Bake at 350°F for 1 hour, or until the potato skin is crispy.
3. When cooled, cut the potato in half. Scoop out the potato from the skin, and fork-mash if desired.

Cheesy Twice-Baked Potatoes

Twice-baked potatoes are a popular dish for the entire family, and a great way to use up leftover baked potatoes. When cooking for the rest of the family, you might add bacon crumbles and diced green onion on the potato before rebaking, and also add a dash of salt and pepper.

YIELDS 2 SERVINGS
1 russet potato
1 ounce shredded Cheddar
1 tablespoon cream cheese
½ tablespoon butter

1. Scrub the potato thoroughly with a vegetable brush. Cut out any bad spots.
2. Pat the potato dry with a paper towel; then poke 8–10 holes into the potato, using a fork or other sharp implement. Bake at 400°F for 1 hour.
3. Once the potato has cooled, slice it open and carefully remove the potato flesh.
4. Mix the potato flesh with the Cheddar, cream cheese, and butter. Stir well, then put it back inside the potato shell. Bake at 350°F for another 15–20 minutes.
5. Slice into strips before serving, or remove the potato skin entirely. Fork-mash if desired.

Toddler Cordon Bleu

When making a stuffed chicken or stuffed beef dish, a meat mallet is important because it will both flatten and tenderize the meat. Simply place the meat on an appropriate work surface, and pound it with the mallet.

YIELDS 2 SERVINGS
1 small boneless, skinless chicken breast (about 6 ounces)
2 thin slices ham
2 ounces cheese, shredded
1 tablespoon butter, melted
2 tablespoons bread crumbs

1. Preheat the oven to 350°F. Wash the chicken breast and remove any skin or fat.
2. Slice the chicken breast in half horizontally. Pound with a meat mallet to make the chicken as thin as possible.
3. Place the ham slices over one piece of chicken. Sprinkle the cheese on top; then place the other piece of chicken on top.
4. Place the assembly in a greased baking dish. Brush with the melted butter and sprinkle the top with the bread crumbs. Bake for 40 minutes, or until the chicken's internal temperature reaches 170°F. The juice from the chicken should run clear when pricked with a fork.
5. Allow to cool, cut into small pieces, and serve.

Mini Meatloaf

Kids love things that are just their size. These pint-sized meatloaves are perfect single-serve foods for toddlers, and the leftovers make great school lunches.

YIELDS 4 SERVINGS
¾–1 pound ground beef
1 egg
½ cup milk or water
3 tablespoons ketchup
2 teaspoons Worcestershire sauce
½ teaspoon oregano
½ teaspoon parsley
Dash of salt and pepper
½ cup bread crumbs
½ small onion, diced
½ cup Cheddar, shredded

1. Preheat the oven to 350°F.
2. In a medium bowl, mix the ground beef, egg, and milk together. Stir well.
3. Add in the ketchup, Worcestershire, oregano, parsley, salt, pepper, bread crumbs, and onion. Mix thoroughly to combine, using your hands if necessary.
4. Scoop equal portions into 6 muffin cups of a metal muffin tin.
5. Bake for 35–45 minutes, or until the meat is no longer pink. About 15 minutes before they're done, sprinkle Cheddar cheese on top of each mini meatloaf. Allow to cool before slicing and serving.

Creamy Chicken and Potatoes

This simple, creamy dish combines cubes of chicken and potatoes with a creamy, cheesy sauce. Just the thing for your child to practice using his new fork on!

YIELDS 4 SERVINGS
1 small potato, cubed
1 cup water
4 teaspoons butter or margarine
2 teaspoons all-purpose flour
½ cup milk
½ cup cooked chicken, cubed
2 tablespoons grated cheese

1. Peel the potato and cut into cubes. Place the potato in a pot with the water. Bring to a boil, reduce the heat, and simmer until tender, about 10–15 minutes. Remove from the pot and drain.
2. In a small pan, melt the butter over low heat. When melted, stir in the flour until well mixed. Add the milk and whisk until smooth.
3. Cook over low heat, stirring often, until the sauce begins to thicken.
4. Add the potato and chicken. Stir for about 3 minutes until all ingredients are heated through.
5. Remove the pot from the heat. Add the cheese and stir until melted. Cool to lukewarm and serve.

Turkey with Fruit*

Turkey fruit salad is a fun way to get kids to eat their protein and vegetables, all in one serving, and you can use up left-over turkey in the process! Adjust the seasonings as necessary to suit your child's taste.

YIELDS 1 SERVING
2 large lettuce leaves
½ cup cooked turkey
¼ cup grapes
¼ cup cantaloupe or honeydew melon
1 ounce mozzarella or Cheddar, shredded
1 teaspoon olive oil
1 teaspoon white wine vinegar
Dash prepared mustard

1. Tear the lettuce into small pieces and place in the bottom of a serving bowl.
2. Cut the turkey into small pieces, removing any fat and skin. Place on top of the lettuce.
3. Wash the grapes and cut in half. Cut the melon into small cubes. Mix grapes and melon in with the turkey.
4. Top with the shredded cheese.
5. Prepare the dressing by mixing the oil, vinegar, and mustard. Stir well; then drizzle over the salad and mix gently.

Sweet-and-Sour Meatballs

If your meatballs always fall apart when you cook them on the stovetop, add a little oil to the pan to keep them from sticking and falling apart. Also, adding more egg and bread crumbs (and pressing the meat very firmly into balls) will keep them from disintegrating into meat sauce.

YIELDS 2 SERVINGS
¼ pound ground beef
¼ cup bread crumbs
½ teaspoon soy sauce
2 teaspoons oil
½ cup canned pineapple chunks, diced
1 teaspoon cornstarch
2 tablespoons water
¼ cup bell pepper, diced

1. Mix the ground beef, bread crumbs, and soy sauce together. Form into 1-inch balls.
2. Heat the oil in a skillet. Add the meatballs, reduce the heat to medium, and cook until the meatballs are no longer pink.
3. Put the pineapple chunks and juice (about ¼ cup) into a small bowl. Add the cornstarch and water, and stir well to mix. Add in the bell pepper.
4. Pour the pineapple mixture into the skillet. Stir the meatballs around to coat in the sauce, and cook the sauce for several minutes or until it thickens.
5. Allow to cool before serving.

Chicken, Pasta, and Carrots

This recipe is a classic spring dish, and one that covers nearly the entire food pyramid! Farfalle pasta is a good choice, but any small pasta shape will cook quickly and be easy for self-feeders.

YIELDS 2 SERVINGS
1 small boneless, skinless chicken breast (about 6 ounces)
2 teaspoons oil
1 medium carrot
½ cup pasta
½ cup chicken stock

1. Wash the chicken breast and remove any skin or fat. Cut into small pieces.
2. Heat the oil in a skillet. Add the chicken; then stir-fry for 10–12 minutes, or until the chicken is cooked.
3. Wash and peel the carrot; slice into thin coins.
4. Bring water to a boil. Add the carrots and cook for about 10 minutes. Add the pasta and cook for another 20 minutes, or until both pasta and carrots are tender.
5. Drain; add the pasta and carrots into the skillet with the chicken. Add the chicken stock and cook at a high temperature for 4–5 minutes.

Mini Pizza Faces*

Bring a smile to your child's face with this smiling pizza meal! You can do any number of substitutions here—olives instead of pepperoni or green pepper instead of carrots. Use whatever vegetables you have on hand.

YIELDS 2 SERVINGS
1 baby carrot
2 tablespoons peas
2 cups water
1 English muffin
2 tablespoons tomato sauce
4 thin slices pepperoni
1 ounce shredded mozzarella

1. Preheat the oven to 375°F.
2. Slice the baby carrot in half lengthwise. Place it and the peas in a saucepan with the water. Bring to a boil; then cook for about 10 minutes, or until the vegetables are tender. Drain and set aside.
3. Split the English muffin in half and lay the two pieces face-up on a baking sheet. Spoon the tomato sauce over each muffin to cover it and lay a foundation for the pizza face.
4. On each muffin, place 2 pieces of pepperoni for eyes. Place half a baby carrot for a nose. Make a smile out of peas. Place the shredded mozzarella around the top of the muffin for hair.
5. Bake for 10–15 minutes, or until the cheese melts.

Creamed Tuna on Toast

Creamed tuna is a quick, easy meal suitable for children of all chewing abilities. If toast doesn't tickle your child's fancy, try serving with crackers or breadsticks. Try adding a touch of sugar or salt if your toddler is balking at the taste. You can also make this meal more visually appealing by adding a handful of peas for color. Be careful about serving tuna too often because of the amount of mercury in it.

YIELDS 1 SERVING
1 tablespoon butter
1 tablespoon all-purpose flour
½ cup milk (regular or soy)
¼ cup chunk light tuna
1 piece whole-grain bread, toasted

1. Melt the butter in a small saucepan.
2. Add the flour, stirring constantly until dissolved. Add the milk and continue stirring until it forms a thick sauce.
3. Turn off the heat and add the tuna. Stir until mixed and creamy.
4. Serve on top of a piece of whole-grain toast.

Fish-Potato-Broccoli Pie

Most toddlers have difficulty with hard pie crust, so this "pie" recipe is minus the shell. Baking it in muffin tins provides single servings and easy leftovers.

YIELDS 6 SERVINGS
1 boneless fillet whitefish
1 cup water
2 medium red potatoes, diced
1 medium carrot, diced
½ cup broccoli, diced
1 tablespoon butter
1 tablespoon all-purpose flour
½ cup milk (regular or soy)

1. Rinse the fish fillet and remove all bones. Cut into small pieces.
2. Bring the water to a boil in a medium saucepan. Add the potatoes, carrot, and broccoli; cook for about 10 minutes. Add the fish and cook another 10–15 minutes, or until the fish flakes easily. When cooked, drain and return the fish and vegetables to the saucepan.
3. In a separate small saucepan, melt the butter. Stir in the flour. Once mixed, add in the milk and stir constantly until a thin sauce is formed. Mix this sauce in with the fish and vegetables, stirring to combine.
4. Divide the fish and vegetables into a 6-cup muffin tin. Bake at 350°F for 30 minutes. Let cool before serving, and fork-mash if desired.

Carrot and Squash Soup

The soup can also be made a little richer by substituting a cup of milk for the vegetable stock. If you're having a struggle peeling the squash, bake it in the oven before combining with the other ingredients.

YIELDS 5 SERVINGS
½ small butternut squash
1 tablespoon butter or margarine
½ small onion, diced
1 small clove garlic, minced
2 medium carrots
6 cups water or vegetable stock
⅛ teaspoon oregano, crushed
⅛ teaspoon thyme, crushed

1. Peel the squash, remove the seeds and pulp, and cut into chunks.
2. Melt the butter in a large saucepan. Add the onion and garlic, sautéing until the onion becomes translucent.
3. Add the squash, carrots, and vegetable stock. Bring to a boil; then add oregano and thyme. Reduce to a simmer and cook for 1–2 hours, or until the vegetables are tender.
4. When the soup is done, purée in a food processor or blender before serving.

Vegetable Soup*

Vegetable soup is one of the most flexible recipes out there. Use chicken, vegetable, or beef stock for added flavor—black beans or chickpeas instead of kidney beans are acceptable substitutes as well. Clean out your vegetable drawer while creating several healthy meals for your toddler!

YIELDS 3 SERVINGS
½ cup green beans
1 tablespoon butter or margarine
½ small onion, diced
1 medium red potato, diced
1 medium carrot, diced
½ cup kidney beans, cooked
Dash of salt and pepper
4 cups chicken stock or water

1. Snap the ends off the green beans, and then cut into 1-inch segments.
2. Melt the butter in a large saucepan. Add the onion, and sauté until it becomes translucent.
3. Add the potato, carrot, green beans, kidney beans, salt, pepper, and chicken stock. Bring to a boil, and simmer for at least 1 hour. Longer cooking will make the vegetables more tender and enhance the flavors, but 1 hour is the minimum cooking time.
4. If desired, fork-mash the vegetables before serving.

Cauliflower with Cheese

Cauliflower may not be everyone's favorite vegetable, but don't let that prejudice prevent you from serving it to your toddler. Serving it up with melted cheese is a perfect way to encourage him to try a new taste.

YIELDS 1 SERVING
½ cup cauliflower
2 cups water
2 ounces cheese

1. Wash the cauliflower, dice into small florets, and place in a steamer basket. Fill the bottom of a saucepan with the water, place the steamer basket inside, then bring to a boil. Cook for 15 minutes, or until the cauliflower is tender.
2. Melt the cheese in a microwave-safe bowl. Heat in the microwave in 30-second intervals, stirring in between, until well melted.
3. Place the cooked cauliflower in a bowl and pour the melted cheese on top.

Pasta and Broccoli

Go as easy (or as heavy) on the garlic as your toddler seems to like. You can easily use part of a clove, or an entire clove if she seems to like it. This is also a perfect dish for serving to the rest of the family, and it won't require any additional seasonings.

YIELDS 2 SERVINGS

½ cup broccoli

4 cups water

1 cup pasta

1 teaspoon olive oil

½ clove garlic, minced

1 teaspoon parsley

1 teaspoon grated Parmesan

1. Wash the broccoli and dice into small florets.
2. Bring the water to a boil. Add the pasta, and cook for about 10 minutes. Add in the broccoli and cook for another 10 minutes, or until both pasta and broccoli are tender. When cooked, drain.
3. Heat the olive oil in a medium skillet. Add the garlic and parsley, sautéing for 2–3 minutes.
4. Add the pasta and broccoli to the saucepan. Sauté for 2–3 minutes, tossing the pasta and broccoli together with the garlic.
5. Sprinkle with the Parmesan before serving.

Chicken with Apricots

One way to save time with this recipe is to use canned apricots instead of fresh. Since canned apricots already have a fair amount of juice, you can also omit the preserves. Simply take 3–4 apricot halves and about a tablespoon of juice, dice into small pieces, and pour on top of the chicken before baking.

YIELDS 2 SERVINGS
1 small boneless, skinless chicken breast (about 6 ounces)
1 apricot
1 tablespoon apricot preserves
½ tablespoon butter

1. Wash the chicken breast and remove any skin or fat. Place in the bottom of a greased baking dish.
2. Dice the apricot into small pieces. Mix with the apricot preserves, then spread over the chicken.
3. Dot the top of the chicken with the butter, then bake for 30 minutes, or until the chicken's internal temperature reaches 170°F. The juice from the chicken should run clear when pricked with a fork, and the chicken meat should not be pink when sliced.
4. Allow to cool; then dice into small pieces for your toddler to self-feed. You can also fork-mash if desired.

Great for Snacks
Sweet Potato Fries

The moisture content of sweet potatoes is very high and often makes very soggy fries. The blanching, panko coating, and parchment paper all help to prevent soggy fries. One last tip: Make sure to not crowd the baking sheet with too many potatoes. If they are too close, they steam each other and then become soggy.

YIELDS 4 CUPS
4 sweet potatoes, peeled and cut into matchsticks
Large bowl of ice water
2 egg whites
⅛ teaspoon garlic powder
1 cup panko Italian-seasoned bread crumbs

1. Preheat the oven to 450°F.
2. Bring a large pot of water to a boil. Place the potatoes in the boiling water and cook for 5 minutes. Drain and immediately plunge into the bowl of ice water. Dry the potatoes well.
3. Combine the egg whites and garlic powder.
4. Toss the potatoes with the egg white mixture and then dip the potatoes in panko bread crumbs.
5. Line a baking sheet with parchment paper, place the fries on it, and bake for approximately 14 minutes.
6. Turn once, about 7 minutes into cooking.

Baked Tortilla Chips

Use whole-wheat tortillas instead of corn for an interesting variation.

YIELDS 40 CHIPS
5 corn tortillas
Canola oil spray
Sprinkle of sea salt

1. Preheat the oven to 350°F.
2. Cut the tortillas into 8 wedges each.
3. Spray a large cookie sheet with the canola oil.
4. Spread the tortilla wedges on a cookie sheet in a single layer. Spray the tops of the tortilla wedges with oil and sprinkle with salt.
5. Bake for 13–15 minutes, until golden and crispy.

Cheese Squares

Baked cheese squares are a delicious way to get some extra protein in your child. Be patient while this finger food is baking—it may take longer than you think.

YIELDS 4 SERVINGS
3 ounces mozzarella, Cheddar, or Monterey jack cheese
1 egg
1 cup all-purpose flour
1 cup cottage cheese

1. Preheat the oven to 350°F.
2. Shred the cheese into a medium bowl.
3. Add the egg, flour, and cottage cheese. Stir well.
4. Place into a greased baking dish.
5. Bake for about 45 minutes, or until a toothpick inserted into the middle comes out clean. Cool and cut into squares.

Simple Hummus

Hummus is a classic Middle Eastern dish that can be served on a variety of things: pita, toast, a cracker, or even a finger. Tahini is a Middle Eastern sesame-seed paste. You can find it in a can in the international or Middle Eastern food section of your grocery store. Once you open the can, mix it well. Refrigerate after opening.

YIELDS 2 SERVINGS
1 clove garlic, optional
1 cup canned chickpeas
1 teaspoon olive oil
1 tablespoon tahini
1 teaspoon cumin
1 teaspoon lemon juice
1 tablespoon water

1. If using garlic, peel it.
2. Rinse the precooked chickpeas. Place in a food processor or blender and purée completely. Add the garlic and purée until well chopped and smooth.
3. Add the olive oil, tahini, cumin, and lemon juice. Continue puréeing for about a minute, scraping down the sides of the bowl as necessary.
4. Add enough water to make a smooth paste. Purée until smooth.

Asparagus Cheese Dip

Asparagus dip is a great way to use up leftover asparagus. This dip is high in vitamin C, vitamin K, and folate, which is beneficial for your toddler's cardiovascular system. Whole-wheat crackers and bread crusts make excellent tools for dipping.

YIELDS 1 SERVING
2 asparagus spears
2 cups water
½ ripe avocado
1 tablespoon cottage cheese

1. Bring the asparagus and water to a boil in a shallow saucepan. Steam for 10–15 minutes, or until the asparagus is soft.
2. Cut the avocado in half. Remove the pit and scoop the avocado out of the skin. Cut into chunks and place into a food processor or blender.
3. When the asparagus is cooked, chop into pieces and add to the food processor.
4. Add the cottage cheese to the food processor and purée until the mixture is smooth. If it's too thick, add cooking water from the asparagus, 1 tablespoon at a time.
5. Serve as a dipping sauce. Refrigerate the leftovers immediately.

Banana-Grape Yogurt Dessert*

While grapes are a choking hazard for the under-one crowd, toddlers can eat grapes as long as they are sliced into halves or quarters. Let your little one self-feed these sorts of fruits, so she can regulate how much she puts in her mouth at a time. As always, supervise!

YIELDS 1 SERVING
½ banana
¼ cup seedless grapes
¼ cup yogurt

1. Peel the banana, removing any brown spots, and cut into thin coins.
2. Wash the grapes and slice into quarters.
3. Combine in a bowl with the yogurt on top.
4. Let your toddler self-feed under careful supervision.

Baby's Peach Cobbler

Traditional peach cobbler is a baked fruit dish with a sweet biscuit topping. Because most toddlers wouldn't be able to eat the topping once it's baked and hard, here's a variation on an old favorite, and one that's tailored right to your child's developing abilities.

YIELDS 2 SERVINGS
1 fresh peach
1 teaspoon brown sugar
⅛ teaspoon cinnamon
½ cups water
⅛ cup rice powder

1. Preheat oven to 350°F.
2. Wash the peach and cut into thin slices. Remove the skin.
3. Place the peach into a small greased baking dish with brown sugar and cinnamon. Give it a quick stir; then bake for 30 minutes, or until the peaches are completely soft.
4. In a small saucepan, bring ½ cup of water to a boil. Add the rice powder and stir for 30 seconds. Cover the pot, turn down the heat to low, and simmer for 7–8 minutes, or until the rice is a smooth, thick consistency. Stir occasionally to prevent sticking.
5. When the peach is cooked, fork-mash. Mix in the cooked rice cereal until the cobbler reaches the desired consistency.

Baked Apples

For the older children, make a caramel sauce from butter and brown sugar; then pour it inside the apple with raisins or cinnamon candies. Serve with ice cream.

YIELDS 1 SERVING
1 apple
1 teaspoon white sugar
⅛ teaspoon cinnamon
¼ cup water

1. Preheat the oven to 350°F. Wash the apple. Remove the top core, leaving the apple intact.
2. Sprinkle the sugar and cinnamon on the inside of the apple. Pour the water into a small baking dish, then place the apple in the center. Bake for about 45 minutes, or until the apple is completely cooked.
3. When cooled, fork-mash to a suitable consistency. If desired, the entire skin can be removed once the apple is cooked.

Fresh Fruit Salad*

Fruit salad is one of the true joys of summer. And the best part: You can substitute any of the ingredients with whatever is in season. Provide a combination of flavors, colors, and textures.

YIELDS 3 SERVINGS
1 kiwi
¼ cup strawberries
¼ cup blueberries
¼ cup raspberries
½ small mango
½ cup seedless grapes

1. Wash the kiwi well and trim off both ends. Slide a tablespoon between the fleshy fruit and the peel. Run the spoon around the entire edge and the fruit should slide out intact. Cut into small pieces.
2. Wash the berries and remove any stems. Cut the strawberries into quarters. Blueberries and raspberries can either be served whole or, if they're large, cut in half.
3. Remove the skin and pit from the mango. Slice into small pieces.
4. Wash the grapes and slice each in half.
5. Combine all fruits in a small bowl, and refrigerate until ready to use. Fork-mash if desired.

Melon Bowls with Yogurt*

Just about any small melon can be used for this recipe, and it's a fun one for small children to help prepare. Allow your child to scoop out the melon seeds with a spoon or an ice-cream scoop, and encourage her to eat the yogurt directly from the melon. Start her out on a road to healthy eating!

YIELDS 2 SERVINGS
1 small cantaloupe or honeydew melon
½ cup blueberries
1 cup yogurt

1. Slice the melon in half. Slice a small piece of shell off the bottom so that the melon will sit easily on a plate.
2. Scoop out and discard all seeds.
3. Wash the blueberries well, sort out any damaged berries. If using large berries, cut each in half.
4. Fill the hollow in the melon with the yogurt. Top with berries.
5. If your toddler has trouble scooping the melon out, assist by removing pieces using a melon baller or grapefruit spoon.

Potato Salad

Potato salad "dressing" can be made in any number of ways. For young eaters, go for simple ingredients, and fewer of them. Also, stay away from heavily seasoned, spiced, or salty variations, and avoid adding little bits of hard celery or pickles that toddlers could choke on. Stick to soft, easily recognizable ingredients.

YIELDS 2 SERVINGS
2 red potatoes
4 cups water
1 tablespoon mayonnaise
1 tablespoon yogurt
½ teaspoon sugar
½ teaspoon prepared mustard
Dash of garlic powder
Dash of salt

1. Wash and peel the potatoes. Cut out any bad spots; then dice into small pieces.
2. Place the potatoes in a medium saucepan and cover with the water. Bring to a boil and cook for 25–30 minutes, or until the potatoes are soft.
3. Drain the potatoes and allow to cool.
4. In a small bowl, mix the mayonnaise, yogurt, sugar, mustard, garlic powder, and salt. Gently toss with the potatoes.
5. Chill before serving. Fork-mash if desired.

Yogurt Fruit Drink*

Here is a healthy summer drink. It could even be made into a winter drink! Simply substitute whatever fruit is in season—it's hard to go wrong with puréed fruit and yogurt. If you're out of fruit, use fruit juice instead.

YIELDS 2 SERVINGS
2 strawberries
1 peach
½ banana
1 cup vanilla yogurt

1. Hull and clean the strawberries. Cut in half.
2. Wash and peel the peach. Remove the pit; cut into pieces.
3. Peel the banana and remove any damaged spots. Cut into chunks.
4. Place the strawberries, peach, banana, and yogurt in the blender. Mix until a thin drink results.
5. Add water as needed, 1 tablespoon at a time, if too thick.

Chickpea and Tomato Salad*

Garbanzo beans, also called chickpeas, are a great staple for toddlers because they're mild in flavor and high in protein. Cooking the chickpeas won't make them much softer, so be sure to fork-mash thoroughly. Cooking the tomatoes will soften them, so feel free to cook them for 10–15 minutes before using.

YIELDS 2 SERVINGS
½ cup canned garbanzo beans
½ cup tomato
1 teaspoon olive oil
1 teaspoon red wine vinegar
½ teaspoon sugar
¼ teaspoon lemon juice
1 tablespoon parsley

1. Drain the garbanzo beans and rinse well.
2. Wash the tomato and remove the stem and any tough white flesh. Dice into small pieces.
3. In a small bowl, mix together the oil, vinegar, sugar, and lemon juice.
4. Toss the dressing with the garbanzo beans, tomatoes, and parsley. Fork-mash before serving. If your toddler seems averse to the sourness of the vinegar, either omit it or skip the dressing entirely.

Cheesy Corn Nuggets

Sometimes known as fritters, corn nuggets are usually deep-fried, but can be made healthier by pan-frying in a small amount of oil. These fried delights, when made with buttermilk and cornmeal, are also called hush puppies.

YIELDS 4 SERVINGS
1 cup canned corn or 3 ears fresh corn, cooked
1 egg
2 tablespoons flour
½ tablespoon butter, melted
¼ cup shredded Cheddar
2 tablespoons oil

1. Shave the corn kernels off the ears of cooked corn, yielding 1 cup of corn kernels. Mash them well with a fork or run them through the food processor.
2. Whisk the egg in a medium bowl. Add the flour, melted butter, shredded cheese, and corn, mixing thoroughly to combine.
3. Heat the oil in a frying pan. When hot, drop the batter into the pan by the spoonful, leaving enough space between them so that the fritters do not touch.
4. Fry 2–3 minutes; then flip over with a spatula. Cook another 2–3 minutes, flipping again if necessary.
5. Drain on paper towels. Serve as finger food once cooled.

Berry Smoothie*

Feel good about serving your child a super-healthy beverage. The yogurt has acidophilus and other live cultures to aid a happy tummy, and berries (particularly blueberries) are known for their potential cancer-fighting abilities. Bananas are in most smoothie recipes because they help with the texture—they make a smoothie thicker and creamier than it would be with only yogurt. Without banana, a smoothie would be more of a slushie, or an iced fruit drink.

YIELDS 2 SERVINGS
½ ripe banana
2 large strawberries
¼ cup raspberries or blueberries
¼ cup apple juice
½ cup yogurt (regular or soy)

1. Peel the banana and remove any damaged spots. Cut into slices and place in a blender or food processor.
2. Wash the berries and remove all stems. Cut in half and place in the food processor. You can use either frozen or fresh berries.
3. Add the juice and yogurt.
4. Blend until the drink is completely smooth.
5. Refrigerate any leftover drink immediately.

Basic Chocolate Chip Cookies*

The nice thing about this recipe is that you can sneak in the healthy nutrition of whole grains by adding powdered oats. For really soft cookies, try using corn syrup instead of sugar.

YIELDS 6 SERVINGS
½ cup shortening
⅓ cup white sugar
⅓ cup brown sugar, packed
1 egg
¾ cup all-purpose flour
¼ teaspoon salt
½ teaspoon baking soda
1 cup ground oats
1 cup chocolate chips

1. Preheat the oven to 350°F.
2. In a medium bowl, cream the shortening and sugars together. Mix with a fork until large crumbles are formed, or use an electric mixer.
3. Add the egg and mix well. Add in the flour, salt, and baking soda, continuing to stir until a dough is formed.
4. Add the oats and chocolate chips. Stir well; then drop spoonfuls onto a greased baking sheet, leaving about 2 inches between each cookie. Bake for 11–14 minutes.
5. Let cool on the baking sheet for 1–2 minutes, then remove and finish cooling on wire racks.

Pear Pudding

Here's an unusual pudding, made with fresh or canned pears, that provides a healthy snack or dessert for your toddler. If you like a crunchy topping on your pudding, try sprinkling graham cracker crumbs on top before baking.

YIELDS 2 SERVINGS
1 medium pear
1 egg, separated
1 teaspoon lemon zest
½ teaspoon cinnamon
2 tablespoons sugar
3 tablespoons all-purpose flour
2 tablespoons milk (regular or soy)

1. Preheat the oven to 375°F. Wash and peel the pear. Remove the stem and seeds, and grate the pear flesh.
2. Place the egg yolk in a bowl. Beat in the lemon zest, cinnamon, and sugar. Mix in the flour and milk; then stir in grated pear.
3. Whip the egg white to soft peaks using an electric mixer. Beat on high until, when you lift one of the beaters out of the bowl, the egg whites form small white peaks. Fold the egg white into the pear mixture.
4. Pour into a greased baking dish. Bake for about 30 minutes or until the pudding is set.
5. Allow to cool before serving.

Chocolate Pudding

Chocolate pudding is as basic as it gets, and it is a favorite when all other mealtime foods seem to flop.

YIELDS 2 SERVINGS
1 ounce unsweetened chocolate
1 tablespoon butter
1 cup milk
¼ cup flour
½ cup sugar
1 egg yolk
¼ teaspoon vanilla extract

1. Put the chocolate and butter into a microwave-safe dish. Microwave on low, in 30-second intervals, until the chocolate is melted. Stir well after each microwave interval to see if the chocolate is sufficiently melted.
2. Combine the melted chocolate and milk in a medium saucepan. Stir in the flour and sugar. Heat almost to boiling, and reduce heat to a simmer. Cook for 5–6 minutes or until the pudding starts to gel together.
3. Give the pudding a good stir, and add the egg yolk. Stir well, then continue cooking over low heat for 2–3 minutes. Stir constantly to keep lumps from forming.
4. Remove the saucepan from the heat. Add in the vanilla and mix thoroughly.
5. Allow to cool before serving.

Strawberry Ice Pops

If you don't have plastic molds, try using disposable paper cups to make this summertime treat. Insert a Popsicle stick once the pop is partially frozen; then simply peel off the cup when it's time to eat.

YIELDS 4 SERVINGS
4 large strawberries
1½ cups water
½ cup orange juice

1. Purée the strawberries in a food processor or blender.
2. Add the water and orange juice to the food processor and mix until completely combined.
3. Pour into a rack of 4 ice-pop molds. Freeze for at least 5 hours before serving.

Creamy Fruit Popsicles

Not sure you want your child having all the additives commonly found in store-bought creamy Popsicles? Make your own! While you can substitute soy milk for cream in this recipe, it doesn't freeze as well, so the end result will be a little icier than a dairy Popsicle.

YIELDS 4 SERVINGS
1 peach, diced
1 cup water
½ cup heavy whipping cream

1. Place the peach in a food processor or blender. Purée completely.
2. Add in the water and cream. Continue puréeing until the mixture is smooth.
3. Pour into a rack of 4 ice-pop molds. Freeze for at least 5 hours before serving.

Apple Nut Bake*

Here's an easy recipe that makes good use of leftover apples. Any variety will do. If using Granny Smiths, you may want to add a pinch more sugar. If your apples are already sweet enough, feel free to omit the sugar entirely.

YIELDS 2 SERVINGS
2 medium apples
4 cups water
¼ cup almonds
1 egg
1 teaspoon all-purpose flour
1 teaspoon sugar
Dash of nutmeg
Dash of cinnamon

1. Preheat the oven to 350°F. Wash, peel, and core the apples. Dice into chunks.
2. Bring the water to a boil in a medium saucepan. Add the apple chunks and cook for 20–25 minutes, or until the apples are tender. Drain the apples and fork-mash into a rough purée.
3. Place the almonds in a food processor or food mill. Grind until they are finely chopped.
4. Mix the apples, almonds, and egg together in a bowl. Add the flour and sugar, stirring to combine. Add the nutmeg and cinnamon, and stir until the mixture is thoroughly coated.
5. Place in a greased baking dish and bake for 30 minutes. Allow to cool before serving.

Peanut Butter Goodies*

Treat your child's sweet tooth with this no-bake recipe. You can mitigate the health concerns by adding a tablespoon of wheat germ to these peanut butter goodies. Also, instead of chocolate chips, try throwing in a few "twigs" of an oat bran cereal.

YIELDS 8 SERVINGS
½ cup graham crackers
3 ounces semisweet chocolate
1 tablespoon shortening
1 cup powdered sugar
½ cup peanut butter
¼ cup chocolate chips

1. Place the graham crackers in a sealing plastic bag. Crush with your hands or a mallet to make coarse crumbs (this is a great task for toddlers).
2. Put the chocolate and shortening into a microwave-safe dish. Microwave on low, in 30-second intervals, until the chocolate is melted. Stir well after each microwave interval to see if the chocolate is sufficiently melted.
3. Mix the chocolate and sugar together until they're combined. Stir in the peanut butter.
4. Add the graham cracker crumbs. Mix gently until they are completely incorporated. Add the chocolate chips and stir until thoroughly mixed.
5. Press into a loaf pan; then cut into cookies about 1" x 2".

Apple and Sweet Potato Mini Muffins

Because these muffins aren't too sweet they're great as a take-along snack, warmed and topped with butter or honey.

YIELDS 42 MINI MUFFINS
2 cups white whole-wheat flour
1½ teaspoons baking powder, divided
½ teaspoon salt
½ teaspoon cinnamon
½ cup applesauce
½ cup flaxseed meal
¼ cup canola oil
½ teaspoon vanilla extract
½ cup milk
1 cup frozen apple juice concentrate
1½ cups grated sweet potato
1 cup grated apple

1. Preheat the oven to 350°F.
2. In a medium bowl, combine the flour, 1 teaspoon of the baking powder, salt, and cinnamon.
3. In a large bowl, combine the applesauce with the remaining ½ teaspoon baking powder.
4. Add the flaxseed meal, oil, vanilla, milk, and apple juice concentrate. Stir to combine.
5. Slowly mix the dry ingredients into the wet.
6. Mix in the sweet potato and apple.
7. Pour the batter into a lightly oiled mini muffin pan.
8. Bake for 25–30 minutes, or until a toothpick inserted into the middle of a muffin comes out dry.

Resources

Books for Your Toddler

Barrett, Judi. Illustrated by Ron Barrett. *Cloudy with a Chance of Meatballs*. New York: Aladdin Paperbacks, 1982.

Breeze, L., and A. Morris. *This Little Baby's Bedtime*. New York: Little Brown, 1990.

Bridwell, Norman. *Clifford the Big Red Dog*. New York: Scholastic Books, 1963. (There are many other *Clifford* books.)

Brown, Margaret Wise. *Goodnight Moon*. New York: Harper Festival; board edition, 1991.

——. *The Runaway Bunny*. New York: Harper, 1942.

Carle, Eric. *The Very Hungry Caterpillar*. New York: Philomel, 1994.

Christelow, Eileen. *Five Little Monkeys Jumping on the Bed*. New York: Clarion Books, 1998.

Eastman, P. D., illus. *Are You My Mother?* New York: Random House Books for Young Readers; board edition, 1998.

Frankel, Alona. *Once Upon a Potty*. New York: HarperCollins, 1999.

Gomi, Taro. *Everyone Poops*. New York: Kane/Miller Book Publishers, 1993.

Keats, Ezra Jack. *Goggles!* New York: Viking, 1998.

———. *Peter's Chair*. New York: Viking, 1998.

———. *The Snowy Day*. New York: Viking Books; board edition, 1996.

———. *Whistle for Willie*. New York: Puffin Books, 1977.

Kingsley, Emily Perl. *I Can Do It Myself*. New York: Western Publishing Co., Inc., 1980.

Kunhardt, Dorothy. *Pat the Bunny*. New York: Golden Books; reissue edition, 2001.

Martin, Bill Jr., and Eric Carle. *Brown Bear, Brown Bear, What Do You See?* New York: Henry Holt and Company, 1983.

Paterson, Bettina. *Potty Time*. New York: Grosset & Dunlap, 1993.

Potter, Beatrix. *The Tale of Peter Rabbit*. New York: Frederick Warne & Company, 1902.

Rey, Margaret, and H. A. Rey. The *Curious George* books. Boston: Houghton Mifflin, 1941–2003. There is a PBS Curious George cartoon series.

Sendak, Maurice. *Where the Wild Things Are*. New York: HarperCollins, 1988.

Dr. Seuss. *Dr. Seuss's Sleep Book*. New York: Random House, 1962.

———. *Fox in Socks*. New York: Random House, 1965.

———. *Green Eggs & Ham*. New York: Random House, 1960.

———. *Hop on Pop*. New York: Random House, 1963.

———. *One Fish Two Fish Red Fish Blue Fish*. New York: Random House, 1981.

Viorst, Judith. Illustrated by Ray Cruz. *Alexander and the Terrible, Horrible, No Good, Very Bad Day*. New York: Aladdin Paperbacks, 1987.

Westcott, Nadine Bernard. *I Know an Old Lady Who Swallowed a Fly*. New York: Little Brown & Co., 1988.

Books for Parents

Brazelton, T. Berry. *Touchpoints: Your Child's Emotional and Behavioral Development*. Cambridge, MA: Perseus Publishing, 1994.

Douglas, Ann. *The Mother of All Toddler Books*. New York: John Wiley & Sons, 2004.

Eisenberg, Arlene, Heidi E. Murkoff, and Sandee E. Hathaway. *What to Expect: The Toddler Years*. New York: Workman Publishing, 1994.

Faber, Adele, and Elaine Mazlish. *Siblings Without Rivalry: How to Help Your Children Live Together So You Can Live Too*. New York: Avon Books, 1987.

Feldman, Robert S. *Child Development*. Upper Saddle River, NJ: Prentice Hall, Inc., 2001.

Hewitt, Deborah. *So This Is Normal Too?* St. Paul, MN: Redleaf Press, 1995.

Iovine, Vicki. *The Girlfriends' Guide to Toddlers*. New York: Perigee Books, 1999.

Kohl, MaryAnn. *First Art: Art Experiences for Toddlers and Twos*. Beltsville, MD: Gryphon House, 2002.

Margulis, Jennifer, ed. *Toddler: Real-Life Stories of Those Fickle, Irrational, Urgent, Tiny People We Love*. New York: Seal Press, 2003.

Murphy, Jana. *The Secret Lives of Toddlers: A Parent's Guide to the Wonderful, Terrible, Fascinating Behavior of Children Ages 1–3*. New York: Perigee Trade, 2004.

Nathanson, Laura Walther. *The Portable Pediatrician for Parents*. New York: Harper Perennial, 1994.

Osit, Michael. *Generation Text: Raising Well-Adjusted Kids in an Age of Instant Everything*. AMACOM: New York, 2008.

Schiller, Pam. *The Complete Resource Book for Toddlers and Twos: Over 2000 Experiences and Ideas*. Beltsville, MD: Gryphon House, 2003.

Shonkoff, Jack P., ed. *From Neurons to Neighborhoods: The Science of Early Childhood Development*. Washington, DC: National Academies Press, 2000.

Spock, Benjamin. *Baby and Child Care*. New York: Pocket Books, 1976.

White, Burton L. *The New First Three Years of Life*. New York: Fireside, 1995.

Winn, Marie. *The Plug-In Drug: Television, Computers, and Family Life.* New York: Penguin Books, 2002.

Zand, Janet, et al. *Smart Medicine for a Healthier Child.* Garden City, New York: Avery Publishing Group, 1994.

Magazines for Parents

Mothering. *www.mothering.com*

Parents. *www.parents.com*

Parent & Child. *www.scholastic.com*

Parenting. *www.parenting.com*

Organizations and Websites

4 Everything Nancy (*www.4everythingnanny.com*): Learn the ins and outs of in-your-home child care at a website devoted to nannies.

ABC Parenting (*www.abcparenting.com*): Get help on thorny issues like day care, weaning, and potty training. There's also information for parents of multiples and discussion groups for everyone.

Baby Parenting (About.com) (*http://babyparenting.about .com*): Here's a website with great smoothie recipes, potty training tips, and the chance to network with other online moms and dads.

Consumer Reports (*www.consumerreports.org*): Evaluates everything from toddler toys and furniture to the pesticides in store-bought vegetables. Subscribe to the magazine by calling (800) 208-9696, or to the online service by visiting their website.

Disney (*www.disney.go.com*): Check out the activities, music, and stories. Games teach toddlers basic concepts like matching, but the sounds and graphics provide great sensory stimulation whether or not they care to play.

Dr. Sonna (*www.drsonna.org*): Read the online articles and get personal answers to your toddler questions at this website.

Kids Dr. (*www.kidsdr.com*): This site contains a wealth of information on health, nutrition, parenting, and behavior.

National Child Care Information Center (*http://nccic.acf .hhs.gov*): When you want child care information, go for the best at the National Child Care Information Center. It has a searchable database, too.

Parent Center (*www.parentcenter.com*): Here's a site that offers a wealth of tips and how-to's to enhance toddler learning, health, and better behavior.

Parents' Choice (*www.parents-choice.org*): Find out which books, toys, videos, software, and TV shows get the thumbs-up from other parents.

Parents Television Council (*www.parentstv.org*): Parents Television Council Green Light Seal of Approval identifies TV shows that exhibit positive values and/or educational content for families. Phone: (213) 629-9255.

PBS Kids (*www.pbskids.org*): Look for activities based on children's television show characters.

The National Parenting Center (*www.tnpc.com*): Before you buy a children's product, check the recommendations and recalls at the National Parenting Center's Seal of Approval website.

Toy Resources; the following sites are helpful in evaluating toys: Oppenheim Toy Portfolio (*www.toyportfolio.com*), the Toys section of About.com *(http://toys.about.com),* and The Toy Guy, which is part of Time to Play (*www.timetoplaymag .com*).

Sites for Software Programs and Apps

Apple (*www.apple.com*).

Appolicious (*www.appolicious.com*): The developer of Toddler Teasers, apps for two-year-olds and older toddlers.

Duck Duck Moose (*www.duckduckmoosedesign.com*): Educational iPhone apps, including Itsy Bitsy Spider, Fish School, Wheels on the Bus, Baa Baa Black Sheep, and Old MacDonald. There is a link on their site of moms who review and recommend apps for toddlers.

Juice Box Software (*www.juiceboxsoftware.com*).

Kids Source (*www.kidsource.com*): The developers of Jump Start Baby and Jump Start Toddler.

Larry Loveland (*www.larryloveland.com*): Cyberstart for young children, freeware that explores sizes, shapes, colors, and order. Uses a mouse, not a keyboard.

Leapfrog (*http://shop.leapfrog.com/leapfrog/*).

Nick Jr. (*www.nickjr.com*): Online games, such as Dora the Explorer, Thomas the Tank Engine, Winnie the Pooh, and Finding Nemo.

Story Place (*www.storyplace.org*).

Story Reader (*www.storyreaderbooks.com*): Books with sound accompaniment, encouraging very young children to read.

Index

304

We Have
EVERYTHING
on Anything!

The Everything® list spans a wide range of subjects, with more than 500 titles covering 25 different categories:

Business	History	Reference
Careers	Home Improvement	Religion
Children's Storybooks	Everything Kids	Self-Help
Computers	Languages	Sports & Fitness
Cooking	Music	Travel
Crafts and Hobbies	New Age	Wedding
Education/Schools	Parenting	Writing
Games and Puzzles	Personal Finance	
Health	Pets	